The Stark Truth With Robert Stark: A Legacy
2009-2018


Edited by Francis Nally

Choam Charity Publishing #004
Philadelphia, PA USA

ISBN-10: 0-9989203-3-9
ISBN-13: 978-0-9989203-3-7

First Edition,
First Printing, 2018

Printed in the USA.

Front cover by Monster Basement:
https://twitter.com/MonBasementArt
https://monsterbasementblr.tumblr.com

"Well let's put it this way, lately I have been listening to tons of ROBERT STARK, in a total Robert Stark phase. And though Robert often talks to White Nationalists, he often talks to Anarchists and Social Creditists and Third Way people and just general Truthseekers. But you're never quite sure what Robert Stark Himself "IS" other than "A Journalist" who likes talking to real interesting people. And his skill is in getting the interesting people to say really interesting things.

Heh. I apologize to Robert, when I first started listening to him I thought he sounded "Spergy" and that his voice sounded funny and awkward and that he had no personality. Well I was dead wrong about that! Plus he has come a long way in sounding less awkward! But he makes people feel comfortable talking to him, and he's real good at probing them. A lot of times he isn't even asking direct questions, but he still gets the people to respond to him as if he was.

Plus he is obviously Sympathetic to a lot these people's causes to actively seek them out and have huge interviews with them like this. But he is never obnoxious or arrogant or pushy towards them. I get the sense he is excited to have A Learning Experience by talking to them.

Bottom line, listen to Robert's show, go back and listen to his old shows on Reason Radio, If you talk shit about Robert Stark you're just an asshole and that's that."

– bkctmoapghow (blogger)

*The man, the legend.*

# ROBERT STARK: AN INTRODUCTION

You've probably heard of Robert Stark because you bought this book and want to know more about him. Otherwise, someone gave you this book so you can learn more about him. Or you just discovered this book in someone's collection and just opened it up and you are now reading this passage.

The problem is, he is as mysterious as this book.

Robert Stark, in nearly a decade, has produced close to 600 radio shows, both live and prerecorded, and released them over the internet. He classifies himself as an "American journalist." Yet with a name so simple like "John Doe," his fame is still unrecognized. Who is he?

A strange, mentally disturbed man that helped create what we know as the Alt-Right.

…That's exactly what the news media said when he had David Duke on his show back in 2012.

Yet Stark had changed his show's direction two years later, when the corrupted Voice of Reason Radio Network went down. Stark at that age was discovering himself.

He was known as a man with a deep alarming voice about "Zionism," "freedom," and "constitutional rights," something you might hear out of Alex Jones.

But ironically, Stark himself loves Jewish culture. Why then in the past was he so self-hating about the idea of some Jewish world order when he actually loves talking about Alicia Silverstone?

This is exactly the most interesting part of Robert Stark. He is an outsider artist that was once used for the forces of trailer park neo-nazism, but now a free man that has broken away from that abuse and records his own social development.

In other words, he is both the Wesley Willis and Lord Haw-Haw of online radio shows (now called "podcast" since things are prerecorded).

I came across Stark during the years surfing Voice of Reason. It's how I also found out about fringe subjects like esoteric fascism, and Jim Goad. Stark's rival during that time was Keith Preston with his own show, Attack The System. It was about anti-liberal anarchy, which sounds very appealing to a crowd that didn't want to feel guilty for liking white nationalism. In essence, associating oneself with white nationalism in 2008-2012 was still considered "queer." The old "white nationalism 1.0" was based upon James Mason, William Pierce, Tom Metzger, and shock jock motorcycle madness. Robert Stark and Keith Preston were the "young" people that would advertise the scene similar to punk rock. Robert Stark in 2010 had on Andrew Yeoman, a leader of a once popular movement that called themselves "national-anarchist." That scene, promoted by Troy Southgate, was like a far-right AntiFa project. That scene is now dead and we have the more politically correct "identitarianism." There is a forgotten association that the alt-right once came from self-destructive queer culture.

And what did Robert Stark have to say about this? Nothing. Because he himself is queer. Not sexually (maybe), but deviant in nature. A true and authentic character that liberals get upset over. Or, "autistic men who live in their mother's basement recording radio show about fringe activists."

But, dear reader, is Robert Stark really a bad person? Or are you appalled and no longer interested reading further about this man's legacy? Again, he has recorded close to 600 radio shows from subjects not only on the far-right, but as well also from the blogging sphere who are critical of the liberal paradigm. Stark will get anyone on his show, from people who he likes on Facebook to girls who he wants to sleep with.

Just remember, Robert Stark had on Richard Spencer before he was the cool guy, as well as Luke Ford and Jack Donovan, who are artist in their own respect. If someone is cool now, Stark had them on first. How did he get them on? Because he has an eye for these things. Because he himself is more queer than the liberal professor you look up to.

I became involved with The Stark Truth when I sent Robert an email about Bratt Sinclaire. Eventually, I got him on, and I became Stark's co-host. Robert Stark is dependent. He relies on others to do his work for him. Yet if you teach him which way to go, he will eventually do what he wants to do, and it's very weird.

Success is determined by how much work and independence you have. Stark could care less about work and "independence," and does his own thing. Sometimes I get mad at his childish antics about women he desires and jokes about homonationalism. I get that he wants to stir up trouble on his show to get more ratings (and frankly, I think he wants to see everything die). I am still good friends with Robert and continue to support him even though he is mentally unstable. But I feel like I have influenced him in a way that is unpreventable.

Mike Connor might have done worse to him almost a decade ago. Luke Ford might have shown him a better way to be happy. And I showed him a way to create art based upon coming-to-age traumas and told him to pursue his desires. The success of The Stark Truth relied on me, and I take responsibility that it is my show too. Although I don't work on it that much anymore, I see Stark learning from his past mistakes and growing.

His show now seems obsolete in an age of fake YouTube celebrities, livestreams, and organized Alt-Right pop culture. Stark still lives in the dark ages where live, pre-recorded radio shows were a thing. That fringe aspect of getting on "haters," is still with him. Like Luke Ford, I am not so sure if Stark really believes what half his guest say.

This book is meant to celebrate Robert Stark's radio show. This is a resume, and published proof of his success. It is a journal about his decade long intellectual growth and his influence upon others.

The next page will cover an intensive interview with Robert Stark, like a documentary film. It is followed by an ultimate checklist of his recorded shows from February 2009 to April 2018. Also included are his rare "Examiner.com" articles that were once advocated by Voice of Reason, three written transcripts of interviews he wrote, and a two-page review of Robert Stark's film, "The Poet and The Cat" by James J' O Meara. Brandon Adamson, a friend of Robert's, writes the Afterword.

If you are still reading this, great. Robert Stark is a fascinating character and this book is an introduction to his work and legacy.

I encourage every reader to listen to ALL Stark Truth shows ever recorded. Please use the checklist in this book (turn to page 33) as a grocery list "to do" guide. You cannot understand Robert Stark until you have listen to 80% of all shows he has ever recorded. Also try to deconstruct his literature in this book to find out who he really is.

The interview on the next page is the start of an intellectual journey you will undergo.

-FN.

# AN INTERVIEW WITH ROBERT STARK.

*The following is an interview (June 2018) conducted with Robert Stark to reflect back on his life and the legacy of The Stark Truth program.*

**Francis Nally:** Where were you born and raised?

**Robert Stark**: I was born and raised in Los Angeles, California.

FN:          What was your childhood like?

RS:          It was fairly atypical.

FN:          How atypical?

RS:          Can you rephrase that?

FN:          Typical, how typical was it?

RS:          Just played with friends, I lived in a small apartment, nothing that unusual.

FN:          What did you want to be when you grew up?

RS:          I think I wanted to be an architect.

FN:          Do you have a middle name?

RS:          Austin.

FN:          Did you ever go to college?

RS:          Yes.

FN:          What college?

RS:          Santa Monica City College and Santa Barbara City College.

FN:     What did you major in?

RS:     Art and theater.

FN:     When did you start getting into politics?

RS:     Around 2008 with Ron Paul.

FN:     Did you publish anything online during the 2008 election?

RS:     I used to write for a website called examiner.com.

FN:     Why did you publish your writings on the now-defunct examiner.com?

RS:     I didn't know it was defunct, but first of all, I got paid for it and it was a great way to get ideas and opinions out there about current events.

FN:     Were you active in 2008 or did you do any radio shows during that time?

RS:     I did some blogging around 2009. I also did some streaming for this defunct network. It was a video site but as well a conservative site.

FN:     What was 15 minutes of freedom on Freedom Broadcast Network about?

RS:     Just some conservative type network.

FN:     Did you apply to it?

RS:     I had a friend who was hosting and he got me on there.

FN:     It's interesting because a lot of those people seem to be old-school libertarians. Would

2009 be your first introduction doing a radio show and acting?

RS:     I would say so, yes.

FN:     What envisions and ideals did you have for the show?

RS:     It inspired me to want to do my own show and to be more independent. The things is they had, the people who ran that network, they have their own political agenda, and it was a little bit different than what I wanted to do.

FN:     Because you would eventually go on Voice of Reason Radio Network?

RS:     That's correct.

FN:     How did you get on VoR?

RS:     Was it Facebook I met Mike Conner online? Was Facebook around back then?

FN:     I think it was, yeah.

RS:     Yeah, I must have met Mike Conner on Facebook or some other social media site, and I got into radio.

FN:     What was Mike Conner like?

RS:     Yeah, he was a really nice guy. Really great to work with. I think he put in too much work. He got overwhelmed.

FN:     I mean, VoR was the first time you really started doing live broadcasting. What was it like broadcasting your show live three days a week during that time?

RS: Well, I did have to do a lot of preparation, but since back then, like right now I edit all my shows and I write up the outlines. Mike Conner was doing all that, so I just had to focus on just recording the shows. They actually weren't technically live. Some shows on that network were live, but I can prerecord a show and Mike Conner would do the editing, and then it was played later.

FN: Interesting because I always that it was live because there were those actual commercial bumps. I didn't know. So, every show was actually prerecorded?

RS: Most of them were. I think I may have done a few. There was a Friday night show with Mishko Novosel that was, Mishko and Dietrich that was live, and people could call in, but my show is prerecorded.

FN: I remembered tuning in live to your shows on Voice of Reason thinking that they were live, and I could have influence just tuning in to the show, but yeah, that's actually very interesting. Did you use Skype back then as well?

RS: Yes, I did.

FN: What was your favorite guest during those times?

RS: I think the most entertaining would be Robert Lindsay, and the most prestigious would be Congressman Jim Traficant.

FN: You became good friends with Robert Lindsay, did you ever meet him in person?

RS: Yeah, I met him twice in Fresno. We ate at first time was at a Filipino restaurant in

Clovis, and the second time was at the P.F. Changs in Fresno with Charles Lincoln.

FN: Did you meet a majority of guest that were on your show during VoR time?

RS: No, I wouldn't say the majority.

FN: Would you say Robert Lindsay would be your favorite guest?

RS: He's the most interesting subject matter. Yeah, he would talk about anything from liberal race realism to POCD.

FN: What happened in late 2012 when VoR started to fail?

RS: Late 2012, Mike Conner quit and he disappeared and then there was that drama with this nut job Carolyn Yeager.

FN: A lot of those VoR guests I remember when you had on your show were actually failed president candidates. I remember Virgil Goode being on your show.

RS: Oh yeah, Virgil Goode, right.

FN: And I actually had the chance to vote for him, but instead I voted for Gary Johnson. Did you have anything to do with getting those candidates on or was it the duty of Mike Conner to get on your guests?

RS: I got most of the guests. Mike Conner got a few of them on.

FN: Did you get people like Virgil Goode and other presidential candidates on the show?

RS:       I think I did. It's been a long time. I forget, but I'm pretty sure I did.

FN:       So, Carolyn Yeager actually ruined VoR?

RS:       Maybe not 100%, but she played a role.

FN:       Did Mike Conner just give up and leave the scene immediately?

RS:       He disappeared and never got the chance to explain why, but that was probably part of it. Part of it was maybe he had personal issues. Maybe he was just overwhelmed of all the work because he was doing everything. He was editing pretty much all the shows. He was doing the streaming, and it's pretty much like a one-man operation.

FN:       There's an interesting gap because after VoR, it stopped, and then Greg Johnson of Counter Currents tried to save Voice of Reason by moving the station onto his website. What's it like during that time?

RS:       Well, Greg Johnson's plan was to recreate Voice of Reason as Counter Currents Radio, and that never fully came into fruition, but for a while he was hosting my show, and I think he briefly also hosted Keith Preston's podcast, Attack the System. So, he had a few podcast running in Counter Currents, but the official plan was to have the Counter Currents Radio and that never came into fruition.

FN:       I remember when Stan Hess had the EUR Hour on Counter-Currents, or something. I remember those days. He also wanted to get Richard Spencer on Counter Currents as well. But yeah, I remember a lot of those shows were happening in 2013. I mean, what were you actually doing during the year of 2013 before you went back to podcasting on Counter Currents?

RS: You mean the space in between?

FN: Yes.

RS: I don't know if I was doing any podcasting because it was a pretty short period of time. I moved over to Counter Currents pretty quickly.

FN: And the Counter Currents phase was very quick and your shows would appear here and there and it seemed like it was the least progressive time during The Stark Truth.

RS: What do you mean? Can you please explain specifically what you mean by that?

FN: I mean, like everyone who was listening three days a week on VoR had to jump on Counter Currents, and it seemed like with the prerecorded nature, shows would just pop up when Greg Johnson would have to upload your newest addition onto Counter Currents.

RS: Oh, I see.

FN: And it seems like 2013 was that year where Robert Stark was missing in action.

RS: Okay.

FN: In fact, it's interesting to know that your first publication is actually on Counter Currents because Greg Johnson transcribed your shows with him, the VoR shows in his book

You Asked for It. How does it feel to be published on Counter Currents?

RS: It's excellent. I mean published my own book, it still feels pretty great to have a transcript out there published.

FN: Yes, it's actually of a time where your show is actually written seriously by someone who's taking it sincere and I think that's very interesting.

RS: Yeah, for sure.

FN: I know there were some instances in the past where you would transcribe shows yourself if the audio is real bad, or the guest only preferred a written interview. What made you feel to go in this direction even though it could take a couple of days just to type out the guest's transcript?

RS: Yeah, that's what it was. There's one issue is the audio quality, and in the case with Robert Lindsay, he actually wrote those transcripts for me, so I didn't have to do the work. With some guests, they prefer the written transcript over using their voice for personal reasons, and that actually wasn't that difficult because I just sent them the questions by email or a Word document and they answered it.

FN: Because it's weird because the show has been a radio show yet there's about three pieces I found online of written transcripts, which I do think even though limited, I think is still interesting. Do you think there's still some value to the written word or would you take the consideration of further writing transcripts or just put that to the side?

RS:        It's too time consuming.

FN:        How did you get in contact of Charles Lincoln?

RS:        William Johnson from the American Freedom Party put me in contact with him because at the time he was living in Los Angeles, West Los Angeles to be specific, and Charles Lincoln was asking to be put into contact with people who were living in the same region.

FN:        He's quite a character.

RS:        He sure is.

FN:        He actually texts me from time to time and you get to know him once you start to conversate with him. He seems like a really good friend for the show.

RS:        Oh yeah. There is a period where it was him and Robert Lindsay on the same shows.

FN:        When did you first register www.starktruthradio.com?

RS:        In 2014.

FN:        I noticed that too. I think I accidentally found it through Counter Currents, and then I realized you're posting such an interview like Dick Smothers Jr. over on your website, and it's odd to think in those terms. Is it a WordPress site?

RS:        Yeah, it's a WordPress site.

FN:        Has the website been more successful than what you've been doing previously on Counter Currents or VoR?

RS: I would say so just because not so much the hit counts, but just because I have my own identity. I mean, I have my own identity back then, but I have a stronger identity because the whole website is devoted to me as opposed to being connected to all these other individuals.

FN: It's like a resume.

RS: Yeah, exactly.

FN: Also, there's a lot of shows you've done with both Matt Forney and some with Andy Nowicki. Both who portray this timid downtrodden character almost like yourself. Any thoughts about them?

RS: I think Andy Nowicki is a great writer. I mean, I especially enjoyed reading his book The Columbine Pilgrim and that had some degree of an influence on in my book. With Matt Forney, I'm a big fan of his earlier writings. I was a big fan of his original site and some of his early book reviews like Mark Ames' Going Postal, but I don't follow him so much anymore.

FN: I always had this vibe that Stark Truth in later years was like the weirdo outcast channel, which now Forney capitalizes on this kind of outsider who's against everything.

RS: The current Stark Truth or the Stark Truth in back then?

FN: I think in most of the period, but I always had this feeling, and especially when you had on Jack Donovan, and then Andy Nowicki immediately came on to write in defense of squares. I felt like with all those

19

shows with Forney and Nowicki it was the start of the antisocial podcast scene.

RS: Oh, yeah for sure.

FN: How did you get in contact with Alex Goldstein?

RS: Over Facebook. I actually found him because he was commenting on Luke Ford's Facebook page.

FN: Luke Ford, he came on during the 2014 time, and actually it's odd to think that Luke was on your show before, he's now doing his own YouTube channel, and he was pretty edgy himself.

RS: Yeah, I mean he still is, but I've done maybe at least five shows with Luke Ford.

FN: So you just sent a message to Alex Goldstein on Facebook?

RS: Yeah, and he was co-hosting the show for quite some time.

FN: I think I remember he would record shows for you using QuickTime or something like that.

RS: Yeah, he did.

FN: Did you ever have long conversations about him with philosophy and things like that?

RS: Yeah. ...Yeah.

FN: I miss him.

RS: Yeah, he's been keeping a low profile and I understand.

FN:     When did you start painting and selling your art?

RS:     I started painting maybe it was around the time I was 15 or younger, and I started selling art commercially when I was about in my early to mid-20s.

FN:     People can donate and buy your paintings through your Facebook page and it's on your website under each podcast, by buying Robert Stark paintings.

RS:     Yes. They should buy them. They should support the show financially.

FN:     And also, you're very interested in photography. Often uploading your photographs of your trips online. Why photography?

RS:     I enjoy traveling and it goes with the whole artistic perspective. I just got back from a trip to Europe, and I should upload those photos.

FN:     What camera do you use?

RS:     Let's see. You know what? I think it's a Sony.

FN:     Have you ever tried using Polaroids?

RS:     I haven't used a Polaroid since I was a kid.

FN:     I notice you did upload some videos onto YouTube about yourself as well as some old ones dating back almost a decade ago. Are you camera shy?

RS:     Camera shy, no.

FN:     Because there is this one video of you
        showing off your artwork, which I think is
        one of the most official and honest Robert
        Stark videos.

RS:     Oh, that was for a class project for a film
        class.

FN:     You also did a short film called The Poet
        and The Cat, and it was actually titled "A
        Robert Stark Production." How did that
        come about?

RS:     Yes. I had Paul Bingham, he wrote the
        script for that, but basically the idea was all
        mine.

FN:     Charles Lincoln is in it too.

RS:     Yeah, Charles Lincoln plays the voice for
        the cat.

FN:     Were you trying to pitch the film to other
        people to make it more in a higher
        production quality?

RS:     I don't know if it will work as a future
        production. It works as a short art film.

FN:     Would you think about doing a short film like
        that again?

RS:     Sure, but my long term goal actually is to
        get my book turned into a film, but that
        would take a lot of funding.

FN:     Did you plan to write Journey To Vapor
        Island when you were a teen?

RS:     No, but it was definitely influenced by my
        adolescent experience, but I planned to
        write Journey To Vapor Island in November

2016, and it took me about a year to write it. Though I came up with the idea a few months before I wrote it.

FN: What parts did Alex Goldstein contribute to the project?

RS: The part about the pills. The green pill, the red pill. His original, actually Alex Goldstein wanted Noam to come out as super masculine when he gets out of prison, but I actually went against that idea, and I had Noam stay himself, his same persona throughout the novel. So, Goldstein's idea, I actually rejected his idea of having Noam come out as super masculine.

FN: I remember that phase, and I remember also our discussions between extreme sex scenes, and dirty jokes. I think those uncut scenes are in the book too. 'm not sure if Brandon Adamson edited out the infamous golden shower scene.

RS: Yeah. He did edit that out.

FN: Fuck. ...One day there'll be a new edition of Journey To Vapor Island, and like William Burroughs' The Naked Lunch, we will have that full scene in there uncensored.

RS: You read the book. How much was edited out from what you got?

FN: I have old files. There was a lot of stuff we wrote, and I think one of my scenes, which made the cut, is the part where Noam has sex for the first time, and we were joking saying that the scene would make a good porno shoot, and it was really awkward and weird. I don't know.

RS: Oh, the part with the actress?

FN: Yeah, and we were actually talking about if we were to make this a live film how would this go about.

RS: Oh, the part where he punches the actress. He can't get a hard and then she insults him and he punches her.

FN: Yeah, that part.

RS: That part!

FN: Do you tell people in person that you have an online podcast show? I remember you once had a roommate, I think it was Gonzales who actually likes your show.

RS: He's not a roommate. I met him because he was a fan of the original Voice of Reason show, but he thinks my shows gotten into to generate, especially on your behalf having you on.

FN: Well, I haven't heard of him since. The only time we talked to him was like, I swear, two years ago?

RS: Oh, you talked to him on Skype with Alex Goldstein?

FN: Yes, and Alex was saying, "Shut up Robert. I want to have a talk with this man." I think. Because Alex Goldstein loves to talk about esoteric Hindu philosophy and tie it in with hipster culture.

RS: He does, yeah.

FN: But again, do you tell people in person to go check out your website?

24

RS:     Sometimes I do. It depends on the person.

FN:     Do you have business cards to say check out my art or shows?

RS:     For my art, not my show.

FN:     Interesting. ...What's with the interest in blonde Jewish girls?

RS:     [laughter] ...I don't know how to explain it. It's just a thing.

FN:     I remember it goes as far back as The Truth Will Live.

RS:     Right, right! Yeah. She hasn't really been active on YouTube anymore, but I remember she used to co-host Luke Ford's original YouTube channel.

FN:     I saw her on Super Chat a few nights ago.

RS:     With Luke?

FN:     Not with Luke, but she just chats, and people know who she is, and I just think it's funny because back then, I'll take with a grain of salt, I would just think it'd be this cool girl on the show, but maybe is there something deeper that she happens to be blonde and Jewish, and like the time you were telling me to get my blonde Jewish girlfriend to be on your show as well.

RS:     Oh, yeah. You were going to do that.

FN:     Do you have Asperger's?

RS:     No, but people have accused me of that.

FN: People seem to look at you as this weird guy that hides behind his computer screen, but talks about deep subjects with fringe celebrities.

RS: Okay.

FN: Yeah, it's often an accusation. Even the idea that you might be a race mixer.

RS: Well, aren't we all?

FN: Do you see yourself as an agitator?

RS: Sure, why not.

FN: Do you like spilling out drama when you do podcasts?

RS: I like to get other people to do my dirty work.

FN: What was one of the most uptight people you've ever had on your podcast?

RS: I've had people cancel. We had that guy we talked to, I'm not going to say his name, but he's a photographer, and he's like, "I looked over your site and I want nothing to do with it."

FN: I mean, yeah you might have one of those people, but I'm talking about the people who you actually had on the show and recorded, and put it up anyway.

RS: I can't think of anyone like that.

FN: For theme songs, the most memorable song I can recall is The Cult, She Sell Sanctuary. Did you ever have any control of that theme song?

RS: I think Mike Conner suggested it, and I liked it. So I went with it.

FN: Who was the guy that said, "This is the Stark Truth with Robert Stark." over that song?

RS: That was Steve from Voice of Reason. Oh, and then for the break music, we had that song ... it was some Italo-disco song.

FN: Tarzan Boy.

RS: Right. Is that Italo-disco?

FN: Yes, it is, and then the ending song, which I always escapes my mind. It's this sad '80s like...

RS: Yeah, I actually forget the name of that song.

FN: And for a while you didn't have a theme song. You would just record it on your end, and say "This is Robert Stark."

RS: Oh, yeah that's when I started the Stark Truth website, and then when I was on Counter Currents, it was this generic, it wasn't really music. It was just this ...

FN: This neo-folk tune.

RS: Oh, yeah. Like da da da da da da da.

FN: But often you will insert your own songs that you will record now, but recently I think FM Attack's Runaway has been the new candidate of the theme song.

RS: Oh, yeah with you doing the voice over.

FN:     I think the first time that it appeared was in the Mark Velard episode, I think.

RS:     Yeah.

FN:     How long will you continue to do your own podcast?

RS:     As long as I'm passionate about the show and as long as I have the time.

FN:     You have gained a cult following over a decade because of the people you have connected with. Is this an Alt-Left movement?

RS:     How do you define Alt-Left?

FN:     Maybe it's like you were once in that growing sphere of the Alt-Right, but now these people are so jaded, depraved and decadent that they're now just, not to say Shock jocks, but at least this new scene where you can be anti-liberal and creative at the same time.

RS:     Yeah, I would say that's accurate.

FN:     Could you call The Stark Truth a movement?

RS:     Yeah. I think the blogger, Aryan Skynet, when he reviewed my book, Journey To Vapor Island, he said something that the subject matter of the show and even an ideology he coined the term "Starkian."

FN:     Did you also meet Brandon Adamson through Facebook?

RS:     Yes, and I've met him in person in Las Vegas.

FN:     Because he's originally the guy who puts out the Alt-Left thing, and it's weird that now, how all of this is interconnected.

RS:     I think it was Robert Lindsay who actually originally coined that term.

FN:     Yes, I think so as well. He had a blog post on it. It's just that Brandon Adamson would go and make the website out of it, and blogs to this day on the subject.

RS:     Yeah, that's correct.

FN:     What do you make of the Alt-Right movement now that it's dying?

RS:     I mean, I did a podcast with Brandon Adamson about the Alt-Right implosion. I think the movement as a whole is just a big mess, it's fallen apart, but there's individual people out there who are doing a great work, great podcast, and great writings and blogs, so I have no idea what's going to happen in the future if something new will emerge, but the Alt-Right has just completely imploded.

FN:     It seems like you made the Alt-Right movement possible, but now as it changed direction, it's a household name. It's almost as if you were the guy that started the Alt-Right accidentally.

RS:     Well, the thing is, I am someone who was loosely associated with the Alt-Right from the very beginning. I was in Voice of Reason before the Alt-Right even became an official thing, but at the same time, I've always stayed pretty much independent. I was never fully in the Alt-Right inner circle, but I've interviewed Greg Johnson before the Alt-Right even existed. I interviewed Richard Spencer pretty early on, so I was connected to a lot of these main figures. I mean, even someone like Tom Sunic. I just recently saw Tom Sunic give a speech in Germany.

FN: Yeah, Tom Sunic is a really good guy as well. People tend to forget these cultural icons now. It seems like today, everyone's now on YouTube and that the prerecorded radio show is something of the past decade. To be up-to-date you have to have a daily show and to get in live viewers and Super Chats, but it seems now what you still do, the prerecorded session and the nature of it being underground, why haven't you moved on to YouTube?

RS: I don't have all the extra time, but I mean that's not the main reason. The main reason is YouTube is just too much censorship.

FN: Would you say Luke Ford is taking your show's concept to a whole new level on YouTube?

RS: I don't know. I think he's doing his own thing. I mean I'm a big fan of Luke Ford's show, but he talks about different subject matter. Like he talks a lot about the JQ. I don't talk about that issue that much.

FN: How would you describe your cultural influence upon, not beyond the Alt-Right, but I guess upon the internet sphere of blogging?

RS: My cultural influence? I've had to ask the people I've influenced. I mean, I think I've definitely influenced a lot of people and a lot of people in this, that you talk about called "the left wing of the Alt-Right" and there is this Starkian sphere, but to answer that question, I have to ask the people who've been influenced by me.

FN: It seems like a lot of young people or at least people who study the Alt-Right don't even know who you are, and yet you've been there for the longest time.

RS: That's true. Paul Bingham was actually saying that I have put out the most content, the most work, the most interesting subject matter, and I don't think I've gotten the recognition that I deserve.

FN: And yet, here we are getting on people who are outside the Alt-Right, but are also artistic and cultural influences, not even knowing your eccentric and controversial past.

RS: Right.

FN: I think that's a key trademark to the Stark Truth where it's just like what Adam Parfrey did with Feral House. Not in it for shock art, but you want to test people's journalism to a whole new level of understanding the arts.

RS: Absolutely.

FN: What piece of wisdom would you give to the struggling artists?

RS: If you have the talent and you believe there's a market out there for your ideas, just put your work out there whether it's visual arts or podcast. I mean the cliché is to say that just be yourself, and it doesn't matter, just work at it, but I'll say if you have a strong confidence in yourself, that you have talent and there's a significant amount

of people out there who can appreciate your
work, then go for it.

**The Complete Stark Truth Checklist 2009-2018.**

This is the complete checklist of every single Robert Stark broadcast published from February 2009 to April 2018. With over 500 listed entries, you may use the following pages as a "checklist" to cross out with a pen which episodes you have listened to. Dates and bold text are provided for significant events. Most shows are available on www.starktruthradio.com, others you have to find on YouTube or through a Google search. To view the Voice of Reason Radio shows, use the link http://www.reasonradionetwork.com through the Wayback Machine to find the original audio files. There is still wild and rare Stark Truth shows out in the wild. ...Can you listen to them all?

## Phase 1: *15 minutes of Freedom* for Freedom Broadcast Network.

Eugene Girin Interview (**The oldest Robert Stark show,** Feb 11, 2009)
My take on the Obama Administration (Apr 10, 2009)
Ted Pike Exposes Hate Crimes Bill & ADL agenda (Jul 1, 2009)
Interview with USS Liberty Survivor Phil Tourney (Sep 28, 2009)
Interview with Chris Simcox (Oct 29, 2009)

## Phase 2: *The Stark Truth* on Voice of Reason Radio Network.

Announcing The Stark Truth with Robert Stark
(**Announced** March 11, 2010)
**The Stark Truth: Debut Show!** (March 25, 2010)
The Stark Truth: AIPAC 2010—High Treason on
Parade (**Mike Connor discussions**)
The Stark Truth: Thoughts on "America"
The Stark Truth: South Africa, Israel & the MSM
The Stark Truth: Interview with Paul Topete (**First
Guest**, Apr 21, 2010)
The Stark Truth: Interview with Phillip Francis Tourney
The Stark Truth: Interview with Phil Tourney & Mark
Glenn
The Stark Truth: Arizona, Machetes, & the Supreme
Court
The Stark Truth: **Interview with Robert Lindsay**
(May 20, 2010)
The Stark Truth: Broadcast with Bob Tuskin
The Stark Truth: Interview with Kievsky
The Stark Truth: Interview with Jim Rizoli
The Stark Truth: Interview with Clayton Douglas
The Stark Truth: The A3P platform
The Stark Truth: Interview with Paul Fromm
The Stark Truth: Robert Lindsay returns
The Stark Truth: Interview with Andrew Yeoman (July
14, 2010)
The Stark Truth: The Tea Party movement
The Stark Truth: Oliver Stone put "in context"
The Stark Truth: Interview with Rev. Ted Pike
The Stark Truth: Interview with James Miller
The Stark Truth: Robert Lindsay on the War on Men
The Stark Truth: Interview with Frosty Wooldridge
The Stark Truth: Andrew Yeoman on Machete protest
The Stark Truth: Interview with John MacArthur
The Stark Truth: **Interview with Matt Parrott** (Sep
22, 2010)
The Stark Truth: Kievsky on men's issues

The Stark Truth: Mass Media & Jewish Pressure
The Stark Truth: Robert Lindsay on advancing White interests
The Stark Truth: Interview with Dennis Mangan
The Stark Truth: Interview with Dennis Mangan #2
The Stark Truth: The Super-rich Oligarchy
The Stark Truth: Interview with Adrian Salbuchi
The Stark Truth: Interview with Keith Johnson
The Stark Truth: Paul Topete returns
The Stark Truth: Interview with Mark Dankof
The Stark Truth: Uprising in the Middle East
The Stark Truth: Frosty Wooldridge Returns
The Stark Truth: Ethnic replacement, Special Interests, and Feminist Decay
The Stark Truth: Interview with David Hamilton
The Stark Truth: The EDL, Muslims, and More on Feminist Decay
The Stark Truth: Dankof on Libya, Muslims
The Stark Truth: **Interview with Keith Preston** (Apr 6, 2011)
The Stark Truth: The Destruction of the Middle Class
The Stark Truth: Our Plutocratic Economic System, Part 1
The Stark Truth: Our Plutocratic Economic System, Part 2
The Stark Truth: Adrian Salbuchi on Debt and Sovereignty
The Stark Truth: Interview with John Médaille
The Stark Truth: AIPAC's Annual Treason Fest, 2011
The Stark Truth: Interview with Dr. Stephen J. Sniegoski
The Stark Truth: News Roundup
The Stark Truth: The Freedom Palooza Festival
The Stark Truth: **Interview with RAMZPAUL** (June 29, 2011)
The Stark Truth: Interview with Yeh Ling-Ling

The Stark Truth: Interview with Max Riekse
The Stark Truth: Interview with William D. Johnson
The Stark Truth: Interview with "Iranian for Aryans"
The Stark Truth: RAMZPAUL Returns
The Stark Truth: RAMZPAUL on the London Riots
The Stark Truth: Keith Preston on Liberty and Populism, Part 1
The Stark Truth: Interview with Virginia Abernethy
The Stark Truth: Keith Preston on Liberty and Populism, Part 2
The Stark Truth: **Interview with Dr. Greg Johnson** (Sep 7, 2011)
The Stark Truth: Matt Parrott on Politics and Strategy
The Stark Truth: Interview with George P. Stimson, Jr.
The Stark Truth: Interview with Reuben Hayat
The Stark Truth: Interview with Patrick McCarthy
The Stark Truth: The Dumbing Down of America (Andrei Kievsky)
The Stark Truth: Interview with Harry Bertram
The Stark Truth: Wall Street Protest & The American Police State (Keith Preston)
The Stark Truth: RamZPaul on Class Warfare & Political Correctness
The Stark Truth: **Interview with Byron Roth** (Oct 7, 2011)
The Stark Truth: Interview with Michael Parish
The Stark Truth: The Ashkenazi Revolution (Reuben Hayat)
The Stark Truth: Interview with Vincent Rinehart
The Stark Truth: Greg Johnson on Occupy Wall Street
The Stark Truth: RAMZPAUL on the "Progressive Stack"
The Stark Truth: Stephen Sniegoski on Interventionism
The Stark Truth: Robert Lindsay on Race, Gender, Cultural, & Personality differences

36

The Stark Truth: Notes from Brett Stevens, Part 1 (Nov 16, 2011)

The Stark Truth: **Interview with James Traficant** (Nov 18, 2011)

The Stark Truth: RAMZPAUL Tames the Shrew

The Stark Truth: Notes from Brett Stevens, Part 2

The Stark Truth: Interview with Dylan Hales

The Stark Truth: RamZPaul on the London Tram Incident

The Stark Truth: Citizens Party Presidential Debate (Keith John Ferguson, Mark B. Graham, Charles Earl Harvey, and Max Riekse)

The Stark Truth: Interview with Siryako Akda (Dec 9, 2011)

The Stark Truth: Interview with William Norman Grigg

The Stark Truth: Interview with Ryu Gaiden

The Stark Truth: Interview with Chuck Rudd

The Stark Truth: RAMZPAUL on Tim Tebow

The Stark Truth: George Stimson Returns

The Stark Truth: Keith Preston on Fascism

The Stark Truth: Interview with Bob Chapman

The Stark Truth: Frosty Wooldridge on Overpopulation

The Stark Truth: Interview with Dick Eastman

The Stark Truth: **Interview with Giovanni Dannato** (Jan 11, 2012)

The Stark Truth: **Interview with Jack Donovan** (Jan 13, 2012)

The Stark Truth: Interview with Sofia Theotoky

The Stark Truth: Interview with Merlin Miller

The Stark Truth: Interview with Tanstaafl, Part 1

The Stark Truth: **Interview with Kerry Bolton** (Jan 23, 2012)

The Stark Truth: **Interview with F. Roger Devlin** (Jan 25, 2012)

The Stark Truth: Interview with Tanstaafl, Part 2

The Stark Truth: **Interview with Andy Nowicki** (Jan 30, 2012)

The Stark Truth: Interview with James Bowery, Part 1

The Stark Truth: Interview with Philip Giraldi

The Stark Truth: Reuben Hayat in Mexico

The Stark Truth: Interview with James Bowery, Part 2

The Stark Truth: **Interview with David Duke** (Feb 10, 2012)

The Stark Truth: Michael Myers on the South Africa Project

The Stark Truth: Robert Lindsay on Masculinity

The Stark Truth: It's Game Over in America (Matt Parrott)

The Stark Truth: Stephen Sniegoski on the Situation in Syria

The Stark Truth: Siryako Akda on the Fifth Freedom

The Stark Truth: Interview with Daniel Carlsen

The Stark Truth: **Interview with E. Michael Jone**s (Feb 29, 2012)

The Stark Truth: Interview with Drake Szekler

The Stark Truth: **Interview with Paul Gottfried** (Mar 5, 2012)

The Stark Truth: South Africa Protest Follow-Up

The Stark Truth: **Interview with Yoav Shamir** (Mar 9, 2012)

The Stark Truth: RAMZPAUL on P.C. Shenanigans

The Stark Truth: Interview with David Husar

The Stark Truth: **Kevin MacDonald on Anti-White Hostility & Israel-First Policing** (Mar 16, 2012)

The Stark Truth: Interview with Winston Wu

The Stark Truth: Greg Johnson on Political Strategies

The Stark Truth: Interview with Lee Whitnum

The Stark Truth: **Interview with John Morgan** (Mar 30, 2012)

The Stark Truth: Greg Johnson on Eco-Fascism

The Stark Truth: Interview with Bill Still

The Stark Truth: Jack Donovan on the Way of Men
The Stark Truth: Interview with Stephen Matthews
The Stark Truth: Interview with Robby Wells
The Stark Truth: **Interview with Kai Murros** (Apr 18, 2012)
The Stark Truth: Andy Nowicki in Defense of Squares
The Stark Truth: Interview with Virgil Goode
The Stark Truth: Interview with Joseph Fasciani
The Stark Truth: Exposé on Ronald Reagan (Mark Weber) (Apr 30, 2012)
The Stark Truth: **Interview with Jared Taylor** (May 2, 2012)
The Stark Truth: **Interview with Anatoly Karlin** (May 4, 2012)
The Stark Truth: Interview with Marc Armstrong
The Stark Truth: Interview with Bromwell Ault
The Stark Truth: Interview with Igor Artemov
The Stark Truth: **Interview with James O'Meara** (May 23, 2012)
The Stark Truth: Interview with Paul Craig Roberts
The Stark Truth: RAMZPAUL on Cultural-Marxist Shenanigans
The Stark Truth: Interview with Ellen Brown
The Stark Truth: Kevin MacDonald on Anti-Immigrant Riots in Israel
The Stark Truth: **Interview with Frank Borzellieri** (June 6, 2012)
The Stark Truth: Interview with David Quintero
The Stark Truth: Conspiracy Theories versus Facts (Mark Weber)
The Stark Truth: Interview with Benjamin Noyles
The Stark Truth: **Interview with Jim Goad** (June 20, 2012)
The Stark Truth: New Right versus Old (Greg Johnson)

The Stark Truth: Interview with Richard Smith (**Last episode,** June 25, 2012)

**Phase 3: *The Stark Truth* on Counter-Currents Radio**

The Stark Truth: Robert Stark **Interviews Mark Weber** on his Iran Trip (Debut, Oct 9, 2012)
Robert Stark Interviews Siryako Akda (Counter-Currents)
Robert Stark Interviews T. J. Parsell
Robert Stark Interviews William van Nostrand
Robert Stark Interviews William Daniel Johnson (Counter-Currents)
Robert Stark Interviews Ramzpaul (Counter-Currents)
Robert Stark Interviews Kevin MacDonald (Counter-Currents)
Robert Stark Interviews Dan Canuckistan
Robert Stark Interviews James J. O'Meara (Counter-Currents, *The Homo and the Negro*)
Robert Stark Interviews Andy Nowicki on Heart Killer
Robert Stark Interviews Anthony Migchels
Robert Stark Interviews Frosty Wooldridge (Counter-Currents)
The Stark Truth: Greg Johnson on Wealth Redistribution (May 18, 2013)
Robert Stark Interviews Andy Nowicki (Counter-Currents)
Robert Stark Interviews Kerry Bolton (Counter-Currents)
Robert Stark Interviews Siryako Akda (Counter-Currents, August 5, 2013)
Robert Stark Interviews Keith Preston (Counter-Currents, August 8, 2013)
Robert Stark Interviews Paul Gottfried on the Frankfurt School (August 12, 2013)

Robert Stark **Interviews Matt Forney** on Going Postal (August 14, 2013)
Robert Stark Interviews Manuel Ochsenreiter on the Syrian Civil War
Robert Stark Interviews Matt Forney on James Burnham, Ann Sterzinger, & Andy Nowicki (October 22, 2013)
Robert Stark Interviews Ramzpaul on Economics (Counter-Currents)
Robert Stark Interviews Keith Preston on the Declining Middle Class & the Rise of Populism
Robert Stark interviews Kerry Bolton on his new book Babel Inc,: Multiculturalism, Globalisation, & the New World Order (Nov 28, 2013)
Robert Stark interviews Greg Johnson on the Boomerang Generation
Robert Stark interviews Greg Johnson on Organic vs. Parasitic Elites & Other Matters
Robert Stark **interviews Charles Lincoln** on the Death of the California Dream
Robert Stark interviews Sri Dharma Pravartaka Acharya on The Dharma Manifesto (Dec 31, 2013)
The Stark Truth: Anthony Migchels Returns to Discuss Monetary Reform
Robert Stark Interviews Monetary Reformer Ellen Brown
Robert Stark Interviews Andy Nowicki (Counter-Currents, Jan 23, 2014)
Robert Stark Interviews Dota from Occident Invicta (Feb 10, 2014)
Robert Stark Interviews Charles Lincoln on the Prison-Industrial Complex
Robert Stark **Interviews Bay Area Guy** from Occident Invicta (Feb 20, 2014)
Robert Stark Interviews Andy Nowicki About His New Novella Beauty & the Least

Robert Stark Interviews Keith Preston (Counter-Currents, March 20, 2014)
Robert Stark Interviews Alexander Jacob
Robert Stark Interviews Alexey Dzermant
Robert Stark Interviews Former Congressman Pete McCloskey
Robert Stark Interviews Professor Albert Bartlett
Robert Stark interviews Greg Johnson on Wealth Redistribution (May, 2014)
Robert Stark Interviews Kerry Bolton on The Banking Swindle
Robert Stark Interviews Matt Forney on The Managerial Revolution
Robert Stark Interviews Andy Nowicki on Lost Violent Souls

**Phase 4: *The Stark Truth* on www.starktruthradio.com**

Robert Stark Interviews Robert Lindsay (Debut, May 21, 2014)
Robert Stark Interviews Winston Wu about American Culture
Robert Stark **interviews Daryl B.** (May 30, 2014)
Robert Stark interviews Keith Preston on The European Elections
Robert Stark interviews Manuel Ochsenreiter on the Ukraine conflict
Robert Stark **interviews Paul Bingham** (June 4, 2014)
Robert Stark interviews Matt Forney on Elliot Rodger, Eroticism & Media Lies
Robert Stark interviews Andy Nowicki about This Malignant Mirage

Robert Stark interviews Dr. William Todd Overcash about Family Court System Corruption (Charles Lincoln)

Robert Stark interviews Kerry Bolton on Peron & Peronism

Robert Stark **interviews David Cole** (June 14, 2014)

Part I: Robert Stark interviews James O'Meara about The Eldritch Evola & Others

Part II: Robert Stark interviews James O'Meara about Houellebecq

Robert Stark interviews Alex from Academic Composition

Robert Stark **interviews Luke Ford** (June 22, 2014)

Robert Stark interviews Dick Smothers Jr. (July 1, 2014)

Robert Stark interviews Matt Forney on Bowden & Sade

Robert Stark interviews Siryako Akda (July 14, 2014)

Robert Stark interviews Joaquin Flores

Robert Stark interviews Bay Area Guy (July 18, 2014)

Robert Stark interviews Keith Preston about Distributism

Robert Stark interviews John Robb

Robert Stark interviews Robert Lindsay on Russia & The Middle East

Robert Stark interviews Daiva Sanda

Robert Stark interviews Max Marco of the Renaissance Party of North America

Robert Stark **interviews Colin Liddell** on the Middle East (August 14, 2014)

Robert Stark interviews Charles Lincoln on Tort Law

Robert Stark interviews Matt Forney on Millennials

Robert Stark interviews Sebastian Ronin (August 28, 2014)

Robert Stark interviews John Robb on Open Source Warfare

Robert Stark **interviews Tom Sunic** on Islam in Europe

Luke Ford is Back! (Sep 3, 2014)

Robert Stark interviews Tom Sunic on the New Right

Robert Stark interviews Andy Nowicki about his Memoir Confessions of a Would-Be Wanker

Robert Stark interviews Richard Spencer (Nov 26, 2014)

Robert Stark interviews Ilana Mercer

Robert Stark **interviews Yoshi Obayashi** (Dec 7, 2014)

Robert Stark interviews Nataliya Kochergova

Robert Stark interviews Paul Gottfried on Dugin & Neoconservatives

Robert Stark interviews Anthony Migchels on the Basic Income

Robert Stark interviews Luke Ford about Nationalism

Robert Stark **interviews Ann Sterzinger** (Jan 11, 2015)

Robert Stark interviews Dota about the Paris Terrorist Attack

Robert Stark interviews Keith Preston about Pan-Secessionist Meta Politics

Robert Stark interviews Luke Ford about Narcissism

Robert Stark interviews Eugene Montsalvat (Mar 3, 2015)

Robert Stark interviews Matt Forney about Tag the Sponsor

Robert Stark interviews Aleksey Bashtavenko about Education

Robert Stark interviews Luke Ford about the Germanwings Pilot, Despair & Eroticized Rage

Robert Stark interviews Ogi Ogas

Robert Stark **interviews The Truth Will Live** (Apr 16, 2015)

Robert Stark interviews Charles Lincoln about A Girl Walks Home Alone at Night

Robert Stark **interviews Jared Taylor** (Robert Lindsay) (Apr 26, 2015)

Robert Stark interviews Luke Ford about how he would feel if he were born into different Outgroups David Cole Returns! (May 3, 2015)

**The Poet & The Cat short film (May 6, 2015)**

Robert Stark interviews Ellen Brown about How America became an Oligarchy

Robert Stark interviews Emril Krestle about Black House Rocked

Robert Stark interviews Charles Lincoln about Las Vegas, New Orleans & Vice

Robert Stark interviews Ramzpaul about the problems of SCALE

Robert Stark interviews Carol Jean Sing / Jerry O'Neil / Charles Lincoln

Robert Stark interviews The Truth Will Live about Cultural & Aesthetic Decline

Robert Stark interviews The Truth Will Live about Cultural & Aesthetic Decline

Robert Stark interviews Luke Ford about Narcissism, Sex Addiction, & Eroticized Rage

Robert Stark interviews Manuel Ochsenreiter about the War of the Idiot

**Robert Stark interviews Rachel Haywire** (The Truth Will Live) (June 1, 2015)

Robert Stark interviews Aleksey Bashtavenko about Introversion & Extroversion

Robert Stark interviews Matt Forney about Social Justice Warriors & Bella and the Bulldogs

Robert Stark interviews Robert Lindsay about the Charleston Church Shooting

Robert Stark **interviews Richard Spencer** about Political Violence & Indentitarianism (July 1, 2015)

Ann Sterzinger Returns! (July 7, 2015)
Robert Stark interviews Ramzpaul about Donald Trump (July 16, 2015)
Robert Stark interviews Robert Lindsay about Personality Types
Robert Stark **interviews Roger Devlin** about Sexual Utopia In Power (July 22, 2015)
Robert Stark interviews Matt Forney about Cuckservatives
Robert Stark interviews Charles Lincoln about Cultural Genocide in the American South
Robert Stark interviews the Truth Will Live about why people become Leftist, Myers Briggs Personality Types & Sexual Morality
Robert Stark interviews Eugene Montsalvat about Alain de Benoist's On the Brink of the Abyss (August 18, 2015)
Robert Stark interviews Dota about Oligarchy & National Capitalism
Robert Stark interviews Robert Lindsay about The Alternative Left, Immigration & Cultural Leftist Insanity
Robert Stark interviews Matt Forney about the Virginia TV Shooting
Robert Stark interviews Bay Area Guy about the SF Bay Area & the Pitfalls of American Exceptionalism
Robert Stark interviews Keith Preston about the Iran Deal, Russia's role in the Mideast, & the US Elections
Robert Stark interviews Colin Liddell about Japan & the European Migrant Crisis
Robert Stark **interviews Richard Spencer** about the European Migrant Crisis & the Trump Phenomenon (Sep 18, 2015)
Robert Stark interviews Luke Ford about Ann Coulter & the Jews
Robert Stark interviews David Cole about Censorship & Selective Outrage

Robert Stark interviews Robert Lindsay about the Oregon Shooter

Robert Stark interviews John Médaille

Robert Stark interviews Andy Nowicki about Notes Before Death

Robert Stark interviews Ellen Brown about Debt & the National Dividend

Robert Stark **interviews Daniel Friberg** (Nov 2, 2015)

Part I: Robert Stark interviews Charles Lincoln about Cities

Robert Stark **interviews Augustus Invictus** (Nov 8, 2015)

Part II: Robert Stark interviews Charles Lincoln about Cities

Robert Stark interviews Anatoly Karlin (Nov 11, 2015)

Robert Stark interviews Bay Area Guy about the Radical Centre

Robert Stark interviews Matt Forney about the NPI Conference, US Cities, Houellebecq, & the Paris Terror Attack

Robert Stark interviews Charles Lincoln about the Paris Terror Attack, Migrant Invasion, & the Middle East

Robert Stark interviews Colin Liddell about Radical Islam & the Black Pill

Robert Stark interviews Roman Bernard about the Paris Terrorist Attack & the Political situation in France

Robert Stark interviews Robert Lindsay about the Turkish attack on the Russian Plane

Robert Stark interviews Paul Bingham about Black House Rocked & Cultural Trends

Robert Stark interviews Luke Ford about the 7th day Adventist Church, Orthodox Judaism & Max Hardcore

Robert Stark interviews Rodrigo Herhaus de Campos

Robert Stark interviews Charles Lincoln about True Stories (Charles sings) (Dec 19, 2015)

Robert Stark interviews The Truth Will Live about Redpilling your family & Catholicism

Robert Stark interviews Sean Gabb

Robert Stark interviews Randall Burns

Robert Stark talks to Charles Lincoln & Robert Lindsay about LA, the 1980's, & Blade Runner

Robert Stark **interviews Rabbit** about the Alternative Left (**Debut appearance**, Jan 9, 2016)

Robert Stark interviews Andy Nowicki about Conspiracy, Compliance, Control, & Defiance

Robert Stark interviews Ann Sterzinger about In the Sky

Robert Stark interviews Colin Liddell about David Bowie

Robert Stark interviews Presidential Candidate Kyle Kopitke

Robert Stark interviews Matt Forney about the Iowa Caucuses

Robert Stark interviews Rabbit about Art, Architecture, & Culture

Robert Stark interviews Ray Sawhill

Robert Stark interviews Keith Preston about Trump & Sanders

Robert Stark **interviews Fernando Cortes** (March 5, 2016)

Robert Stark interviews Bay Area Guy about the case for Economic Populism

Robert Stark **interviews Aleksandr Dugin** (Mar 24, 2016)

Robert Stark interviews Paul Gottfried about his book Fascism: The Career of a Concept

Robert Stark **interviews Alex von Goldstein (Debut appearance**, Apr 2, 2016)

Robert Stark interviews Anatoly Karlin about Radical Centrism, Immigration, Trump & Russia (AG first co-host, Apr 8, 2016)

Robert Stark interviews Presidential Candidate Scott Smith (AG)

Robert Stark interviews Rabbit about Robert Heinlein

Robert Stark interviews Giovanni Dannato (AG) (Apr 28, 2016)

Robert Stark **interviews Ron Unz** about his campaign for Senate (AG) (May 1, 2016)

Robert Stark interviews Thomas Rinaldi about New York Neon (Rabbit as co-host, May 9, 2016)

Robert Stark interviews Bay Area Guy about the New American Civil Wars (AG)

Robert Stark interviews Richard Spencer about the Meme Wars (AG) (May 21, 2016)

Robert Stark interviews Keith Preston about The Tyranny of the Politically Correct (AG)

Robert Stark interviews Rabbit about Futurism

Robert Stark interviews Alex von Goldstein about Pepe the Frog

Part I: Interview with James O'Meara about Green Nazis in Space (R) (AG) (June 11, 2016)

Part II: Interview with James O'Meara about Green Nazis in Space

Robert Stark and Rabbit talk about their trip to Las Vegas (June 21, 2016)

Robert Stark **interviews Zoltan Istvan** (R) (June 26, 2016)

Robert Stark **interviews Charles Krafft** (R) (July 4, 2016)

Robert Stark interviews Keith Preston about the New Political Paradigm (AG)

Robert Stark, Rabbit, & Alex von Goldstein talk about Radical Centrism, Cultural Elitism, & Gore Vidal

Robert Stark **interviews Professor Darrell Hamamoto** (AG) (July, 18, 016)

Robert Stark interviews Alex von Goldstein about Conspiracy Theories & The Green Pill

Robert Stark interviews Richard Spencer about the RNC Convention (AG) (July 23, 2016)

Robert Stark **interviews Peter Brimelow** (AG) (July 28, 2016)

Robert Stark interviews Adam Hengels about Market Urbanism (R)

Robert Stark **interviews Mark Velard** (R) (**Debut of Runaway theme song**, Aug 4, 2016)

Robert Stark, Rabbit, & Alex von Goldstein talk about Future Trends & Scenarios

Robert Stark **interviews Tila Tequila** (AG) (Aug 12, 2016)

Robert Stark **interviews Brandon Adamson** about Beatnik Fascism (AG) (**BA debut,** Aug 18, 2016)

Robert Stark **interviews Richard Wolstencroft** (AG) (Aug 21, 2016)

Robert Stark, Rabbit, & Alex von Goldstein discuss Retro Futurism

Robert Stark interviews Rabbit about Hillary Clinton's Speech & the Alternative Left

Robert Stark interviews Keith Preston about Thinkers Against Modernity (AG)

Robert Stark interviews Ray Sawhill about Journalism (AG)

Robert Stark interviews Laura Foote Clark of Grow SF (R) (Krishan Madan) (Sep 12, 2016)

Robert Stark interviews Scott Jackisch (R)

Robert Stark **interviews James Howard Kunstler** (R) (AG) (Sep 21, 2016)

Robert Stark, Rabbit, Alex von Goldstein & The Truth Will Live discuss Hipster Culture

Robert Stark and Alex von Goldstein discuss the first Trump Clinton Debate

Robert Stark interviews Paul Bingham about Aleister Crowley (AG)

Robert Stark interviews **Haarlem Venison** (AG) (Oct 5, 2016)

Robert Stark talks about his trip to the San Francisco Bay Area (R) (AG) (Oct 8, 2016)

Robert Stark, Rabbit, and Alex von Goldstein talk about the 2nd Presidential Debate, Milo & the Alt Left

Robert Stark talks about Mishima, Taxi Driver, & Aristocratic Individualism (AG)

Robert Stark interviews Jim Goad (R) (AG) (Oct 17, 2016)

Robert Stark interviews Alt Left Blogger Ryan Englund (R) (AG) (Robert Lindsay)

Robert Stark interviews Bay Area Guy about the SF Bay Area and the FIRE Economy (AG)

Robert Stark interviews Director Matthew David Wilder (AG) (Oct 30, 2016)

Robert Stark **interviews Pilleater** (AG) (**Debut appearance**, Nov 3, 2016)

Robert Stark interviews Richard Wolstencroft about Aristocractic Radicalism (AG)

Alt Left Election Roundtable with Robert Stark, Ryan Englund, Bay Area Guy, Rabbit & Alex von Goldstein (Nov 10, 2016)

A talk with Luke Ford and Richard Wolstencroft about Occultism, Nationalism, and the Election of Trump (AG)

Robert Stark interviews Paul Bingham about Wyndham Lewis, Ernst Jünger, & Italian Futurism (AG)

Robert Stark interviews Keith Preston about Donald Trump and the Return of Liberalism (AG)

Robert Stark interviews Pilleater about Music & Manga (AG)

Robert Stark and Pilleater talk about the Film Salò (AG) (Nov 23, 2016)

Robert Stark **interviews Jamie Stewart** from the band Xiu Xiu (Pilleater first co-host, Nov 26, 2016)

Robert Stark **interviews Animator John R. Dilworth** (PE) (Nov 30, 2016)

Robert Stark interviews writer Cameron Pierce (PE)

Robert Stark interviews Joshua David McKenney (PE)

Robert Stark interviews Filmmaker Jim Van Bebber (PE)

Robert Stark interviews Alt-Left Youtuber Prince of Queens about SJW's & the Regressive Left (PE) (Bay Area Guy) (Dec 9, 2016)

Robert Stark interviews Anatoly Karlin about his American Decade, Futurism, & Political Trends (PE)

Robert Stark interviews Robert Inhuman (PE)

Robert Stark interviews filmmaker Christopher Moonlight (PE)

Robert Stark **interviews Jeffrey Mishlove** (PE) (Dec 20, 2016)

Robert Stark **interviews Ronnie Martin** (PE) (Dec 22, 2016)

Robert Stark talks about his trip to LA (PE) (R) (Charles Lincoln)

Robert Stark interviews Charles Marohn from Strong Towns (PE)

Robert Stark interviews Prince of Queens about Economics & the Alt Left Movement (PE) (Bay Area Guy)

Robert Stark interviews Artist Arthur Kwon Lee (PE)

Robert Stark interviews Scott Laudati (PE)

Robert Stark interviews Patalliro fan artist Alex Su (PE)

Robert Stark interviews Netrunner World Champion Dan D'Argenio (PE)
Robert Stark interviews Lynn Zook
Robert Stark **interviews Game Designer Andy Looney** (PE)
Robert Stark interviews Robert Brenner about his Gritty Old Time Square Tours (PE)
Robert Stark **chatters with actor Nicholas Vince** (PE) (First appearance of J.G. Michael) (Jan 16, 2017) (PE)
Robert Stark interviews Comic Writer Woody Arnold (PE)
Robert Stark talks to Anatoly Karlin about his return to Russia and Predictions for 2017 (PE)
Robert Stark talks to Pilleater about Kaze to Ki no Uta, Avant Garde Art, & Philosophy
Robert Stark interviews Italian Artist Shinja (PE)
Robert Stark interviews Ryan Andrews, author of The Birth of Prudence (PE)
Robert Stark **interviews Italian Eurobeat Artist Bratt Sinclaire** (PE) (Jan 26, 2017)
Robert Stark **interviews John Kenneth Press** (PE) (Jan 28, 2017)
Robert Stark **interviews Musician En Esch** (PE) (J.G. Michael) (Jan 30, 2017)
Robert Stark **interviews Jason Reza Jorjani** (PE) (Feb 2, 2017)
Robert Stark interviews Reactionary Tree (PE)
Robert Stark **interviews The Adventure Kid** (PE) (Feb 5, 2017)
The Return of Rabbit! (PE) (Feb 6, 2017)
Robert Stark talks to Ryan Englund about the SJW Riots (PE) (R)
Robert Stark interviews Artist Epiphora (PE)

**A talk with Cosmic Encounter Game Designers Peter Olokta, Greg Olokta, & Bill Elirbie** (PE) (Feb 12, 2017)

Robert Stark interviews Dr. Gleb Tsipursky (PE)

Robert Stark interviews New Retro Wave Artist Robert Parker (PE)

Robert Stark interviews Thom Young (PE)

Robert Stark **interviews Curt Doolittle** (PE) (Feb 20, 2017)

Robert Stark interviews Bay Area Guy about our Rigged Economic System (PE)

Robert Stark talks to Rabbit about the Milo Controversy (PE) (Left of Arbanon) (Feb 24, 2017)

Robert Stark talks about the Film The Crush Starring Alicia Silverstone (PE) (Charles Lincoln) (**Count Fosco**) (Craig Langley Jr.) (Feb 26, 2017)

Robert Stark interviews Constantin von Hoffmeister (PE) (R)

Robert Stark **interviews Count Isidor Fosco** (PE) (Mar 2, 2017)

Robert Stark talks to Rabbit and Greg Johnson about the Alt Left Dilemma, Culture, & Aesthetics (PE) (March 4, 2017)

Robert Stark **interviews Adam Parfrey** (PE) (J.G. Michael) (Mar 6, 2017)

Robert Stark **interviews Musician David Thrussell** (PE) (RW) (Mar 8, 2017)

Robert Stark interviews Darren Toni (PE)

Robert Brenner returns to talk about his Time Square Tours (PE)

Robert Stark talks to Tiffany & James From the Band Fire Tiger (PE)

Robert Stark interviews Italo Disco Artist Andy Fox (PE)

Robert Stark interviews Vincent Law (PE)

Robert Stark talks to Giovanni Dannato about Solutions to Social Problems (PE)

Robert Stark talks to Pilleater about Depech Mode's Spirit Album (John Curley) (Mar 22, 2017)

Robert Stark talks about Clueless, The Babysitter, & The Meme Magic of Alicia Silverstone (PE) (Charles Lincoln) (Count Fosco) (Craig Langley Jr.)

Robert Stark interviews Devotional Dave from STRANGELOVE-The Depeche Mode Experience (PE) (Mar 26, 2017)

Robert Stark **interviews Jasun Horsley** (PE) (Mar 28, 2017)

Robert Stark talks to Pilleater about his Novella "Trip" (Mar 30, 2017)

Robert Stark talks to Bay Area Guy about Trump & The Healthcare Cartel (PE)

Robert Stark talks to Director Matthew David Wilder about Dog Eat Dog & Upcoming Projects (PE)

Robert Stark **interviews Musician Alex Romane** (PE) (Apr 5, 2017)

Robert Stark talks to Rabbit about Trump's Betrayal & Attack on Syria (PE)

Robert Stark, Pilleater, & Richard Wolstencroft discuss Ghost in a Shell (PE)

666D Interuniversal Teichmuller Chess with Anatoly Karlin (PE) (R) (Anatoly Karlin)

Robert Stark interviews Musician Dean Clarke of Brutalist Architecture in the Sun (PE)

Robert Stark **interviews Jay Dyer** about Esoteric Hollywood (PE) (Apr 15, 2017)

Robert Stark **interviews Josh Alan Friedman** (PE) (Apr 18, 2017)

Thomas Rinaldi returns to talk about Neon (PE)

Robert Stark **interviews Leisure Suit Larry Creator Al Lowe** (PE) (R) (Apr 22, 2017)

Robert Stark interviews New Retro Wave Artist Absolute Valentine (PE)

Robert Stark interviews J. David Spurlock about Margaret Brundage (PE)

Robert Stark interviews Frank H. Buckley (PE)

Robert Stark talks to Anatoly Karlin & Guillaume Durocher about the French Election (PE)

Robert Stark interviews Jack Ravenwood (PE)

Robert Stark interviews Filmmaker and Author Pablo D'Stair (PE)

Robert Stark and Pilleater discuss Psychosocialism (May 8, 2017)

Robert Stark interviews Author Ray Harris (PE)

Robert Stark talks to Jim Goad about the New Church Ladies and Re Release of Answer Me! (PE) (Adventure Kid) (May 12, 2017)

Robert Stark **interviews Shaun Partridge** (PE) (May 14, 2017)

Robert Stark talks to Pilleater about Almond Eyes Baby Face (May 16, 2017)

Robert Stark talks to Count Isidor Fosco about creating New Retro Futurist Sub Cultures (PE)

Robert Stark interviews Gustavo Semeria about Argentina (PE)

Robert Stark talks to Anatoly Karlin about Automation & the Basic Income (PE)

Robert Stark interviews Tunnels & Trolls Creator Ken St. Andre (PE) (May 24, 2017)

Robert Stark talks to Brandon Adamson about his Compare and Contrast EP (PE)

Robert Stark and Richard Wolstencroft discuss The Film Dark City (PE) (Count Fosco)

Robert Stark interviews Publisher Josh Dale (PE)

Robert Stark talks to Count Fosco about the Film Blast From The Past (PE)

Robert Stark interviews Jeffery J. Smith (PE)

Robert Stark talks to Jay Dyer about Esoteric Twin Peaks (PE)

Robert Stark interviews Italian Musician and Artist Dino Olivieri (PE)

Robert Stark **interviews Music Composer Dana Countryman** (PE) (Adventure Kid)

Robert Stark **interviews Game Designer James Ernest** (PE) (June 14, 2017)

Robert Stark interviews Santa Barbara Mayoral Candidate Maiza Hixson (PE) (Adventure Kid)

Robert Stark interviews Joseph Dobrian (PE)

Robert Stark talks to Director Richard Wolstencroft about The New Twin Peaks (PE) (J.G. Micheal) (Count Fosco) (June 22, 2017)

Robert Stark **interviews Artist Jason D'Aquino** (June 24, 2017)

Robert Stark talks to Scott Laudati about Cuba & Occupy Wall Street (PE) (Adventure Kid)

Robert Stark interviews Musician Andy Diamond of Diamond Field (PE)

Robert Stark talks to Giovanni Dannato about The Post Scarcity Economy (PE)

Robert Stark talks to Thom Young about Instagram Poetry

Robert Stark talks to Brandon Adamson about the Film Cherry 2000 (PE) (**first appearance of Sam Kevorikian**) (July 8, 2017)

Robert Stark interviews Yan Pagh about the Alt Center (SK)

Robert Stark talks to Director Michael Medaglia about his Film Deep Dark (SK)

Robert Stark interviews Frank Sanitate about a Public Bank for Santa Barbara County (SK)

Robert Stark interviews Joshua Zeidner (SK)

Robert Stark talks to Anatoly Karlin about Transhumanism & Effective Altruism (SK)

Robert Stark interviews Korezaan about Transit & Urbanism (SK) (Bay Area Guy)

Robert Stark talks to Giovanni Dannato about the Alt-Center (SK) (Joshua Zeidner)

Robert Stark talks to Zoltan Istvan about his Proposal for a California State Basic Income (SK) (Aug 1, 2017)

Robert Stark talks to Mike Marinacci about California Jesus (PE) (J.G. Micheal) (August 5, 2017)

Robert Stark talks to Jamie Curcio about Narrative Machines (SK) (J.G. Micheal)

Robert Stark talks to Director Richard Wolstencroft about The New Twin Peaks: Part II (SK)

Robert Stark talks to Joshua Zeidner about The Tech Industry, H-1B's, Surveillance & The Google Memo (SK)

Robert Stark interviews Old Urbanist Charles Gardner (SK)

Round Table Discussion on Charlottesville & Political Polarization (Keith Preston) (SK) (J.G. Micheal) (JZ)

Robert Stark interviews Hank Pellissier (SK) (JZ)

Robert Stark **interviews Manga Artist Toshio Maeda** 前田俊夫 (SK) (JZ)

Alt Left Chaos Magic With Brandon Adamson (SK)

Robert Stark talks to Pilleater about the case for a New Alt-Left (SK) (J.G. Michael)

Robert Stark interviews Musician Jody Coombes of Star Noir (SK) (J.G. Micheal)

Robert Stark interviews Actor and Musician Karim Theilgaard (SK)

Robert Stark interviews Model Charise Jeanine (Joshua Zeidner)

Robert Stark interviews Danish Filmmaker Julius Telmer (SK)

Robert Stark talks to Robert Brenner about HBO's The Deuce and 1970's Time Square (Sep 8, 2017)
Robert Stark talks to Richard Wolstencroft about the Twin Peaks Finale (PE) (Sep 10, 2017)
Robert Stark interviews Jayman (SK) (Joshua Zeidner)
Robert Stark interviews Kevin Lynn of Progressives for Immigration Reform (SK)
Jamie Stewart from Xiu Xiu returns to talk about his album Forget & Twin Peaks (PE) (Haarlem Venison) (RW) (Sep 16, 2017)
Robert Stark talks to Giovanni Dannato about the Mechanisms of Social Status (SK)
Robert Stark talks to Count Fosco about the Mechanisms of the Arts (PE) (Sep 21, 2017)
Robert Stark talks to Director Jonathan Holbrook about his Film Tall Men
Robert Stark talks to Director Jared Shumate about his film Last Night Out (J.G. Michael)
Robert Stark interviews Synthwave Artist Damokles (SK) (J.G. Michael)
Robert Stark interviews Anthony Hamilton (PE) (Debut of new theme) (October 6, 2017)
Robert Stark interviews Transhumanist Andres Gomez Emilsson (**PE as Francis Nally**) (Oct 11, 2017)
Robert Stark interviews Dain Fitzgerald (Joshua Zeidner)
Robert Stark talks to Luke Ford about the Harvey Weinstein scandal (Joshua Zeidner)
Robert Stark talks to Lynn Zook about Gambling on a Dream Volume 2
Robert Stark talks to Richard Wolstencroft about his new film The Second Coming Volume II
Robert Stark talks about his new novel Journey to Vapor Island (FN) (BA) (Nov 22, 2017)

Robert Stark talks to Count Fosco about the show Californication
Robert Stark interviews James Lafond (Paul Bingham) (Jan 11, 2018)
Robert Stark interviews Vaporwave Artist Spear 槍

(FN)
Robert Stark **interviews Rodney Alan Greenblat** (FN) (Jan 30, 2018)
Robert Stark talks to Giovanni Dannato about Alt-Center Neo-Tribalism
Robert Stark talks to Count Fosco about the film Eyes Wide Shut
Robert Stark interviews Ashley Messinger (BA) (Feb 18, 2018)
Robert Stark talks to Director Matthew David Wilder about his film Regarding the Case of Joan of Arc (Count Fosco)
Robert Stark talks to Ashley Messinger about Retro Futurism (BA)
Robert Stark talks to Keith Preston about The Geek Squad & Corporate Surveillance State Collusion
Robert Stark talks to Brandon Adamson about the Alt-Right Implosion (Mar 17, 2018)
Robert Stark talks to Count Fosco about Cruel Intentions, Sex, Class & Alt Politics
Robert Stark talks to Kevin Lynn about his Ad Campaign against H-1B Visas on SF's BART
Robert Stark talks to Ann Sterzinger about her Novel LYFE (Paul Bingham) (Mar 29, 2018)
Robert Stark talks to Francis Nally about his book A Manifesto About Stalking Patrick Hyland (Apr 1, 2018)
Robert Stark interviews Architect Adam Mayer
Robert Stark interviews Linh Dinh (Apr 5, 2018)
Robert Stark talks to Constantin von Hoffmeister about Archeofuturism (BA)

Robert Stark talks to Ashley Messinger about Roger Blackstone & The Politics of AESTHETICS (Apr 11, 2018)
Robert Stark talks to Luke Ford about The Dangers of The E-Personality
Robert Stark talks to Anatoly Karlin about The Syria Strikes, Russian Politics & Failure of Trump (BA)
Robert Stark interviews DECAY about Politics & Urbanism
Robert Stark interviews Peter Moruzzi about Mid-Century Modern (Adventure Kid)
Robert Stark interviews Al Barna and Randall Ann Homan about San Francisco Neon
Robert Stark interviews filmmaker Bjørn Erik Sørensen about his film BROKE (Apr 28, 2018)

# Tolkien versus the Frankfurt School: The Good, the Bad, & the Ugly of the Left

August 15, 2011

I was listening to Tom Sunic's recent interview with Counter-Currents Publishing editor Greg Johnson on the Voice of Reason Broadcast Network, which also hosts my show, *The Stark Truth*. The topic of the interview was the New Right movement in Europe, which has recently made inroads within the American Alternative Right. The New Right differentiates itself from the American conservative movement, which is thought to be based on classical liberalism rather than European traditionalism.

During the interview, Johnson pointed out that,

"A lot of things that are conventionally left-wing by contemporary standards are not so different from things that were defended by traditionalists in Europe. So we tend to have a critical attitude about capitalism. We tend to be opposed to the despoiling of the environment or the destruction of history, [for] walkable communities, [against] processed crappy food and things like that. We tend to be, in many ways in terms of lifestyle and aesthetic taste and things like that, aligned with people that are contemporary leftists, but I would even say that the contemporary Left has roots, if you go back far enough, where things blend together with things that are more right-wing if you will, or let's just say European traditional forms of society.

So one of the things that I talk about is what I like to call "West Coast White nationalism" because West Coast White nationalism, a lot of the people that I know on the West Coast who think in terms of a racially defined new order of society, you take one look at them and you think that they're hippies or you think that they're liberals. Their lifestyles and their attitudes embrace a lot of things like Eastern spirituality, and drinking fruit juice, and wearing sandals, and granola, and vegetarianism, and organic food and organic farming, all these sort of things that you think are kind of hippie things.

If you look at the roots of a lot of the West Coast hippie culture and also the hippie culture in Europe for that matter, a lot of it goes back to Tolkien. What doesn't come from the New Left, let's say the Frankfurt school and things like that, a lot of it comes from Tolkien which is pretty much directly connected with European Traditionalism."

Despite the fact that he lived before the modern environmental movement, Tolkien had a passionate love for nature, which he expressed in his work. He was personally disgusted by the greed and destruction of nature which occurred during the industrialization of Great Britain and often used the term "steward" in his work. There is a book by Matthew T. Dickerson called *Ents, Elves and Eriador: The Environmental Vision of J.R.R. Tolkien*, which examines the message of stewardship of nature in his work. The author examines how the community the Hobbits is sustainable and self-sufficient, as well as how the Ents preserve the forest of Fangorn.

In an essay from 1968 entitled "The Hobbit and the Hippie" on the influence that Tolkien's work had on the hippie movement, co-authors William Ratliff and Charles Flinn point out that "the great respect for the past found in the trilogy has already been noted, and it is this respect which in part supports the rejection of the idea of continual progress. For the hippies, however, continual progress is denied because it conflicts with the exaltation of undifferentiated experience and with the state more usually associated with madness."

While in regards to issues such as preserving the environment there is truth to this, it's obvious that the counterculture movement of the 1960s brought about great societal change, mainly due to the influence of cultural Marxism and the Frankfurt School.

Critics of cultural Marxism have made the argument that it is an ideological tool to subvert traditional institutions and concepts such as Western Civilization, nationalism, Christianity, race, gender, and the family. In his book *Death of the West*, Pat Buchanan asserts that cultural Marxists have taken control of the American media and use it as a tool to infect the minds of Americans. Other traditional conservatives have made similar arguments. William S. Lind stated that "Political Correctness is cultural Marxism. It is Marxism translated from economic into cultural terms. It is an effort that goes back not to the 1960s and the hippies and the peace movement, but back to World War I. If we compare the basic tenets of Political Correctness with classical Marxism the parallels are very obvious." In his book *The Strange Death of Marxism*, Paul Gottfried argues the point that Marxism outlived communism in form of cultural Marxism rather than economics.

While they have vast differences in ideology and values, both Tolkien in his works and the cultural Marxists of the Frankfurt School laid the ideological ground work for the 1960s counterculture movement, which most political thinkers characterize as left-wing. Causes that were associated with the hippie movement include the anti-war, pro-environment, anti-racist, feminist, and anti-consumerist ones. More recently, the Left much like the modern Right has sold out many of their principles to big capital and consumerism; however, the influence of the

Frankfurt School remains and has influenced society though the media and academia.

Today, Hollywood, which is often described by social conservatives as a bastion of liberal elitism, is the perfect example of an unholy marriage between cultural Marxism and consumerism. While Hollywood continues to attack nationalism, Whites, men, Christianity, and the family, it also promotes mass consumption and conformity, despite conning the consumers into thinking they are being edgy. Working for the advertisement industry, Sigmund Freud's nephew, Edward Bernays, who was an avowed cultural Marxist, implemented these ideas, using his uncle's knowledge of psychological manipulation, on unsuspecting consumers. Obviously the main objective of those who run Hollywood is to make money, but even cultural Marxists figure that crony capitalist economics and consumer culture are the best way to make a profit as well as spread their ideas and warp the minds of billions of people throughout the world.

Ironically in response there is now a growing counterculture movement in the alternative Right that has revived a lot of the principles that are associated with Tolkien's work as well as with the original counterculture Left. Greg Johnson, who stresses building a new political coalition that reaches beyond the Left-Right paradigm, wrote in essay titled "West Coast White Nationalism," where he describes this counter culture movement which is primarily found on the West Coast.

He says that he has "noticed that today's West Coast White Nationalists tend to be socially and even politically more left-wing than White Nationalists from other parts of the United States. I'll never forget the evening in 2003 when, at a David Irving lecture in San Francisco, I met a daughter of the '60s counterculture who told me that her two favorite books are *The Lord of the Rings* and *Mein Kampf.*"

He continues to list further characteristics:

- West Coast White Nationalists tend to have higher SWPLQs ("Stuff White People Like" Quotients) than White Nationalists in other parts of the US. (I liked 122/150 SWPL in the first Stuff White People Like book, but only 41/92 SWPL in Whiter Shades of Pale.)

- West Coast White Nationalists tend to be more strongly concerned with environmental preservation, healthy and sustainable lifestyles, and combating animal cruelty than White Nationalists in other parts of the US. If Savitri Devi were alive today, she would be smuggling stray cats into an organic gardening commune in Berkeley.

- West Coast White Nationalists tend to be more critical of the workings of unrestrained global capitalism. We are pro-labor, protectionist, pro-zoning, and pro-small business.

- West Coast White Nationalists tend to be more non-Christian and to be more honest about it than other White Nationalists. I know atheists, agnostics, neo-pagans, New Agers, and even some who have made extensive study and practice of Eastern philosophies and religions. Religious pluralism and tolerance would definitely be features of a West Coast White Republic.

- West Coast White Nationalists tend to be more tolerant of homosexuals, bisexuals, "androphiles," and "none of the aboves" who put their racial identity first.

- West Coast White Nationalists tend to be more tolerant of drugs like marijuana and psychedelics.

- West Coast White Nationalists are far less hung up on sub-racial distinctions and Old World feuds than White Nationalists in the East and South. We tend to think of ourselves as whites first and foremost.

While Johnson is a White nationalist, which of course is not for everyone within the greater conservative movement, Rod Dreher, who is a journalist for National Review, has expressed similar ideas in his book titled "Crunchy Cons," which also discusses this growing counterculture whose belief that "'small is beautiful' often puts them at odds with the mainstream corporate influenced conservative movement." Dreher states "that being a truly committed conservative today" should mean "being as skeptical of big business as you are of big government."

68

# Mexico and Israel Lobby should examine their own immigration policies before condemning Arizona

June 30, 2010

The Anti-Defamation League and the Government of Mexico have filed separate lawsuits against the State of Arizona over its new immigration law which will take effect July 29. Lawyers representing Mexico filled a brief supporting the law suit which was brought by the ACLU which they are taking to Federal Court claiming that the law violates the US Constitution. The document put out by the government of Mexico states that the law threatens "the human and civil rights of its citizens when they are present in Arizona." Mexican President Felipe Calderon has condemned the bill stating it "opens the door to intolerance, hate, discrimination and abuse in law enforcement."

While the Government of Mexico is outraged about Arizona its own immigration laws are far harsher than Arizona's. While Arizona's law calls for the arrest and deportation of illegal immigrants, under Mexican Law, entering the country illegally is punishable by up to two years in prison and an attempted re-entry by up to 10 years. Those who violate their visas can be sentenced to up to six years and the government of Mexico has the authority to arrest foreigners whom it deems as a threat to its national and economic interest.

*[half of this article is missing, sorry]*.

# Populist revolt in primary elections: patriot Paul in; traitor Spector out

May 27, 2010

Primary elections were held across the country on Tuesday and Wednesday. While the last two major elections had a partisan tone, within both the democrat and republican primaries there has been a major backlash against the establishment candidates. Rand Paul, who is the son of Congressman Ron Paul and favorite of the Tea Party Movement, defeated the establishment backed candidate Trey Grayson in the Republican Primary of Senate in Kentucky and Senator Arlen Specter was defeated on the democratic primary by Congressman Joe Sestak.

What we are seeing with this election that has not been seen in a while is that the voters are rejecting the establishment backed candidates. While the Tea Party has been co-opted to some degree, it has given a platform for patriotic Americans toinfluence the result of elections. Rand Paul whose father helped start this movement had the backing of liberty minded Americans across the country. His opponent Tray Grayson had the backing of the entire GOP establishment, including Dick Cheney, but that was not enough to get him nominated.

71

Rand Paul's nomination is a sign for change to come with the GOP. The Hill's John Feehery said "Rand Paul's election may very well mean the beginning of the end of the neo-conservative movement in the Republican Party. It also might mark the beginning of the end of the social-conservative wing of the Republican Party." Mainstream Conservative pundit George Will even admitted his ideas were catching on with Republican voters stating "it may seem strange for a Republican to have opposed, as Paul did, the invasion of Iraq. But in the eighth year of that war, many Kentuckians may think he was strangely prescient. To some it may seem extreme to say, as Paul does, that although the invasion of Afghanistan was proper, our current mission there is "murky." But many Kentuckians may think this is an extreme understatement.

This has caused concern for the Republican establishment. Former Bush speech writer David Frum denounced Paul's victory, stating, "Rand Paul's victory in the Kentucky Republican primary is obviously a depressing event for those who support strong national defense and rational conservative politics. In another year, such a victory would be a prelude to a Republican defeat in the general election." While some of Paul's hardcore supporters are disappointed by his verbal support for Israel, Neocons like Frum are upset that the principles of non-interventionism and opposition to foreign aid are making a comeback within the conservative movement.

Frum acknowledges that Paul's victory symbolized frustration with the Republican establishment stating, "How is it that the GOP has lost its antibodies against a candidate like Rand Paul?" He admits his impact on the GOP adding, "But despite Paul's self-presentation as "anti-establishment," the D.C. conservative establishment by and large made its peace with him. It is this acquiescence – even more than Paul's own nomination – that is the most ominous news from tonight's vote."

Senator Arlen Specter dropped out of the Republican Party because of opposition from the Tea Party crowd. Sestak who had the backing of the anti-war movement will go on to face Republican Pat Toomey who is the Tea Party favorite in the general. Specter was beholden to powerful pro-Israel interest. Morton Klein who was the former head of the Zionist Organization of America said, "Anything I ever asked Arlen Specter to do with respect to Israel or Jews, he has always done it." Klein also credit Specter's role in maintaining foreign aid for Israel. While Toomey and Sestak are no Rand Pauls, they are certainly vast improvements over Specter, who was for amnesty for illegal immigrants, bailouts, foreign aid, and the Iraq War.

In the upcoming primaries many more establishment candidates are vulnerable, primarily John McCain who angered voters will his co-signing of the McCain/Kennedy amnesty bill. He is facing Congressman J.D. Hayworth, who has made border enforcement his signatory issue.

73

Like Specter, McCain supported the bailouts and represents much of the same globalist interventionist agenda.

Paul's victory and Specter's defeat represent a growing movement for national sovereignty and non-interventionism that threatens the powers that be. This is just the beginning, as many other candidates are appealing to this growing populist sentiment against partisan politics and corruption in Washington and Wall Street.

# Joe Lieberman's fascist agenda to strip Americans of their Constitutional rights

May 14, 2010

Senator Joe Lieberman is sponsoring a bill with Massachusetts Republican Scott Brown called the "Terrorist Expatriation Act" that would strip terrorist suspects of their citizenship. The bill applies to any American that supports a foreign terrorist organization or any organization that is deemed a supporter of terrorism by an ally of the United States. The bill gives the State Department the power to determine who is a terrorist, and strip away their citizenship.

Lieberman introduced the bill stating, "The State Department will make an administrative determination... the State Department will now have the authority to revoke their citizenship... they will not enjoy the rights and privileges of American citizenship in the legal proceedings against them.... he could then be tried by military commission as the Unprivileged Enemy Belligerent that he is."

Even though Lieberman claims the bill is to target Americans who have joined Islamic Terrorist Organizations such as Al Qaeda, it has implications affecting many American political dissidents, not just those who one would usually think of as terrorist. Hypothetical scenarios that the bill might apply to are Americans such as former Congresswomen Cynthia McKinney who are helping out Palestinians in Gaza with food and medical aid. Since Israel considers Hamas a terrorist organization and Israel is considered as ally by the US Government.

Another scenario is American Patriots who are helping out the Afrikaner Resistance Movement, which is a secessionist movement in South Africa. Let's say the ANC Government in South Africa declares the movement a terrorist organization and the US state department decides to go after Americans who are helping the organization.

Joe Lieberman also sponsored another bill in the Senate with John McCain called the "Enemy Belligerent, Interrogation, Detention, and Prosecution Act". This bill which has been described as the "Patriot Act on steroids" gives the President the power to determine if an individual poses a terrorist threat so that they can be detained and interrogated. Under this Bill the suspects would lose their Miranda rights and Sixth Amendment Right to an Attorney and fair trial.

McCain explained it stating, "we still don't have a clear mechanism, legal structure, and implementing policy for dealing with terrorists who we capture in the (alleged) act of trying to bring about attacks on the United States and our national security interests at home and abroad."

Lieberman added, "These are not common criminals. They are war criminals. Anyone we capture in this war should be treated as a prisoner of war, held by the military, interrogated for information that will protect Americans and help us win this war and then where appropriate, tried not in a normal federal court where criminals are tried but before a military commission."

These two bills sponsored by Joe Lieberman tie in to each other. One bill strips Americans of their citizenship, and the other of their right to a fair trial once they lose their citizenship. Many conservatives supported the Patriot Act under Bush thinking it would only be against Islamic extremists, but now Obama can use it to go after those in the Tea Parties and the patriot movement who have already been labeled by the establishment as "domestic terrorists".

These bills create a dictatorship where the State Department is given the power the strip the rights of any American citizen, especially political dissidents. Maybe someday when Americans take back their country, this law may be used against the same traitors who are behind this bill who also happen to have ties to foreign terrorists.

# Lies about Zionism and the New World Order from the left and the right

May 10, 2010

**There has been a lot of debate about whether Zionism is nationalism or internationalism from both supporters and critics of Israel. Many leftist critics of Israel view it as a hyper-nationalist state while its supporters have said that it is only trying to defend its national sovereignty. They both agree that Zionism is Nationalism, however the left tends to take the position that nationalism is bad and leads to conflicts and wars.**

The late Howard Zinn who was one of Israel's leading critics on the left in an article titled "Israel was a Mistake" stated "I think the Jewish State was a mistake, yes. Obviously, it's too late to go back. It was a mistake to drive the Indians off the American continent, but it's too late to give it back. At the time, I thought creating Israel was a good thing, but in retrospect, it was probably the worst thing that the Jews could have done. What they did was join the nationalistic frenzy, they became privy to all of the evils that nationalism creates and became very much like the United States-very aggressive, violent and bigoted. When Jews were without a state they were internationalists and they contributed to

78

whatever culture they were part of and produced great things. Jews were known as kindly, talented people. Now, I think, Israel is contributing to anti-Semitism. So I think it was a big mistake."

While many of those on the left see nationalism as the root cause of Zionism's problems, many supporters of Israel have pitched the idea to American nationalists that Israel is a nation whose national sovereignty is under siege by the same globalist elites who are destroying America's sovereignty.

One such individual is Canadian Israeli Journalist Bary Chamish. He is a staunch supporter of Israel but has also aligned himself with the American patriot movement speaking out against the New World Order. In his article titled "New World Order's Control of Israel's Economy" he starts out stating "The forces who wish to create a New World Order (NWO) based on a One World government, long ago realized that to destroy a nation's sovereignty, it was not enough to merely corrupt its diplomacy; they must also enjoy the overwhelming leverage that comes with controlling its economy. So, through the World Bank and International Monetary Fund (IMF), they have planted compliant administrators throughout the governments of the world."

He goes on to talk about how Israel has been victimized by the globalist stating "by controlling the nation's economy, the NWO inherits control of its independent diplomacy. In Israel, in the early 1980s, the NWO retaliated against the honorable and independent Prime Minister, Menachem Begin by shooting the inflation rate up to 450%. The men who arranged this from within the government were Bank of Israel Chairman Michael Bruno and Finance Minister Yoram Aridor. Bruno justified a series of measures by Aridor guaranteed to cause instant inflation, including the sudden and unexpected lifting of most duties on imported goods. Both men were rewarded well for their treachery: Aridor, against all natural reason, was made Israel's United Nations ambassador and Bruno retired to the good life at the IMF." He concludes his article saying "The Chairman of The Bank Of Israel, is possibly the most dangerous individual in the country."

Chamish who admired Begin has also claimed that Ariel Sharon was in cahoots with Henry Kissinger to orchestrate the Sabra and Shantila Massacre in Israel's 1982 War in Lebanon to destroy Begin's reputation. However, it was Begin who was the leader of the 1948 Dir Yasin Massacre against the Palestinians and who said "Our race is the Master Race. We are divine gods on this planet. We are as different from the inferior races as they are from insects. In fact, compared to our race, other races are beasts and animals, cattle at best. Other races are considered as human excrement. Our destiny is to rule over the inferior races. Our earthly kingdom will be ruled by our leader with a rod of iron. The masses will lick our feet and serve us as our slaves."

John Hagee who is an evangelical pastor with a following in the millions and founder of Christians United for Israel has also made similar statements about the globalist trying to destroy Israel. Hagee believes that the Rothschilds and international bankers control the Global economy through the Federal Reserve and are setting up a One World Government. Hagee fails to mentions that it was the Rothschilds who helped financed the creation of the state of Israel, including the Israeli Knesset, and have a major street named in their honor in Tel Aviv.

What is ironic is that Hagee's views about the New World Order are similar to many of those who are considered "anti-Semitic conspiracy theorist" and have even got Hagee himself accused of anti-Semitism by some liberal Jewish organizations despite his staunch support for Israel. However, he claims that these globalist elites want to destroy Israel, successful at appealing to those who believe in the New World but getting them to support Israel rather than involved in anti-Zionism.

In has long been considered an anti-Semitic canard to accuse Jews of being internationalist dating back to Henry Ford's infamous "The International Jew." However, many Jews have discussed the role that Jewish interest have played in promoting Globalization. The Kvetcher who is a Jewish blogger that is very critical of the organized Jewish community responded to a statement by David Duke where Duke said that Americans "are bitter because unelected economic czars such as Greenspan and Bernanke, Wolfowitz and a whole coterie of Jewish "people who aren't like them" have ripped them off and have let so-called "free trade" destroy the American economy." The Kvetcher stated that "the Jewish role in promoting privatization and globalization is large and unfortunate. It is a communal embarrassment." Concluding the article, the Kvetcher says "Does Duke exaggerate a bit? Sure. Is he a conspiracy theorist? Absolutely. But he hits far too closely to the reality far too frequently for any of us to be comfortable with where we are as a community, or for where we have helped push this great country in recent years."

Asher Ginsberg who is considered the ideological founder of the modern Zionist movement argued that Israel should be a spiritual center for all Jews worldwide and disagreed with other Zionist such as Theodore Herzl who's goal was to concentrate the worlds Jewish population in the state of Israel. Historian Dr. Norman Cantor described Ginsberg's vision that would "serve as a foundation in The Holy Land for a Hebrew-speaking cultural center for world Jewry-an elite cultural center for world Jewry."

To this day there are Zionist in Israel who are blood and soil Nationalist but the leaders of the movement are internationalist with dual citizenship who chose not to live in Israel but view it has a safety net in case of an anti-semitic uprising in the West. In the Film about anti-semitism titled "Defamation", Israeli Film Makers Yoav Shamir asked wealthy ADL's donors why they did not live in Israel and they replied that Israel is their insurance policy.

The CFR is the one of the nation's most powerful think tanks who's membership includes every big name in politics and have promoted a North American Union modeled after the EU. Former Congressman John R. Rarick warned that "The CFR, dedicated to one-world government, financed by a number of the largest tax-exempt foundations, and wielding such power and influence over our lives in the areas of finance, business, labor, military, education and mass communication media, should be familiar to every American concerned with good government and with preserving and defending the U.S. Constitution and our free-enterprise system. Yet, the nation's right to know machinery – the news media – usually so aggressive in exposures to inform our people, remain conspicuously silent when it comes to the CFR, its members and their activities."

Besides supporting the erosion of America's sovereignty, the CFR has been devoted to hawkish pro-Israel agenda in the middle east. In 2002 The CFR sponsored a book by Kenneth Pollack titled "The Threatening Storm: The Case for Invading Iraq." Now CFR President Richard Haas is talking about regime change for Iran. He wrote an article titled (Enough Is Enough: Why we can no longer remain on the sidelines in the struggle for regime change in Iran) where he calls for regime change and UN Sanctions against Iran. Haas has also criticized Obama for not being supportive enough of Israel. Elliot Abrams who is the CFR's Senior fellow for Middle Eastern Studies has even advocated for a US military strike against Iran.

Zinn says that Zionism is flawed because it was based on nationalism, while Chamish makes an appeal to western nationalist who's sovereignty is under attack. While Israel itself is not the culprit behind globalism, the internationalist power structure in the United States unconditionally supports Israel and most powerful pro-Israel organizations in the West such as the ADL support open immigration and globalization. Israel is dependent on Western financial and military support which powerful pro-Israel interest groups in America and other Western Nations Lobby for. While in principle Zionism may be nationalism in practice it is internationalism.

# American hero Jim Traficant files for congressional run as an independent

May 8, 2010

Former Democratic Congressman James Traficant who released last year after serving a seven year sentence wants his old job back. On Monday Traficant filed the paper work to run as an independent candidate for in Ohio's 17th District Congressional District, which is currently held by Traficant's former aid Democrat Tim Ryan. About the election, Traficant said "maybe it's time money doesn't dictate an election."

A Book by Michael Collins Piper titled "Target: Traficant" presents evidence that Traficant was framed by the Justice Department. He was set up on false charges of bribery, filing false income tax returns, obstruction of justice, racketeering, and conspiracy to defraud the United States, and was ousted from Congress. He was offered a plea bargain but refused to plea guilty to crimes he didn't commit. Traficant said "they had no physical evidence against Traficant." He added "Seven people said they bribed him. They had no crime against Traficant. They taped every phone call he ever made, probably. Since 1983."

About his experience in prison, Traficant quoted Nelson Mandela stating "if you really want to know the truth about a nation, you've got to go through their prisons," and added "Believe me, he's right. And I learned an awful lot about America going through the prisons." His personal experience behind bars have shaped his views on reforming our nations prison system. He said "these nonviolent offenders.... Instead of spending all that money in prison, send 'em home. You don't need to be in prison in America like this."

While a democrat, Traficant earned the reputation of an independent populist making a lot of powerful enemies within his own party and powerful special interest groups, notably the Israeli Lobby. He was able to win 15% of the vote in 2002 running as an independent despite being in prison. His District is in economic distress due to jobs going overseas and the financial crisis which makes it ripe for Traficant's economic populist message against Unfair Trade deals, illegal immigration, and corruption on Wall Street. Traficant supports the abolition of the income tax and stated that "I want the Internal Revenue Service to look at me very carefully. I plan to throw you the hell out and give Americans some freedom.

Since his release from prison he hosted his own local talk show and has been a frequent guest on shows throughout the country. He was the main speaker at a recent Tea Party and is a popular figure within that movement. However he says that he is not the Tea Party Candidate.

86

Traficant's platform calls for the deportation of illegal aliens, brining

home the troops from overseas and instating them on the border, a flat

25% consumption tax to replace the income tax, and the abolition of the

Departments of Energy and Education. He has the powers that be dead

set against him but he has proved than he is willing to sacrifice his own

personal well-being for his country and the truth.

# Opposition to Arizona immigration bill exposes Neocon hypocrisy

May 3, 2010

The New immigration bill which is by far the toughest in the nation has created controversy. Many of its critics say that the bill amounts to racial profiling and even compared it to Nazi Germany. There are Constitutional concerns that the bill violates the 4th Amendment's right against unlawful search and seizures, because it gives law enforcement the authority to detain those suspected of being in the country illegally.

While it is understandable that the left and civil libertarians would oppose such a bill some of the staunchest criticism of the bill is coming from the same neocons who supported the Patriot Act and other measures to crack down on civil liberties. Fred Barnes of the Weekly Standard and Fox News pundit called the bill "draconian" and says "it goes way too far." George Bush's former political strategist Karl Rove denounced the bill saying "I think there is going to be some constitutional problems with the bill...." I wished they hadn't passed it, in a way."

While he makes legitimate points about the bill he has no credibility considering the fact that George Bush violated the constitution on many occasions such as the Patriot Act which also violates the 4th Amendment, enacted an unconstitutional war, and even said that "The Constitution is just a G_D piece of paper."

Besides prominent Neocons many hawkish Pro Israel organizations such as the Anti-Defamation League, American Jewish Committee, and Simon Wiesenthal Center have also condemned the Bill. The ADL stated it "seduces the people of Arizona with the false promise of improving safety and security in our state, but fails to do either," said Bill Straus, Arizona Regional Director. "In actuality, this bill drives a wedge between local law enforcement and the communities they are sworn to serve and protect. Members of our state's significant Latino and immigrant populations – citizens and non-citizens alike – will hesitate to come forward to report crimes or serve as witnesses. Instead, they will reside in the shadows and law enforcement will lose some of its best partners in the fight to keep our communities safe."

Assaf Oron points out in an article on the blog Mondoweiss titled "Israel has been 'Arizona' all along" that "In Israel, laws like the Arizona one – and worse – have been in effect ever since independence. No, I'm not talking about the Occupation, but inside Israel proper. Any resident sixteen years of age or older must at all times carry an Identity card, and present it upon demand to a senior police officer, head of Municipal or

89

Regional Authority, or a policeman or member of the Armed forces on duty. And guess against which ethnic group this requirement is enforced."

I guess if its good enough for Israel why not Arizona? But much like Karl Rove and Fred Barnes the ADL endorsed the Patriot Act, lobbied for thought crime laws, and was discovered to have a role in the Missouri State Police's targeting of those in the Patriot Movement. It is clear that these individuals and organizations do not care about individual liberties, so what is there incentive for opposing the bill.

In his article titled "MidEast Policy-Immigration Policy: Is The Other Boot About To Drop?" CSULB Prof. Kevin MacDonald points out that "the two issues of Israel and immigration relaxation (in the U.S.) have in common a deep and straightforward Jewish commitment to particular policies. My contention is that both policies have been construed by Jewish leaders as being helpful to the security and political influence of their community."

MacDonald adds "in the case of Israel, this is self-evident. In the case of immigration policy, there ample documentation of a consistent interest by the Jewish community, both in America and in Europe, in ending the hegemony of the host community amongst whom they live. The measures taken to enforce their chosen objectives suggest there is indeed an element of truth in what Foxman dismisses as "the old canard

90

and conspiracy theory of Jewish control of the media, Congress, and the U.S. government".

Besides ethnic motivation among these special interest groups there are other motivations such as corporate and financial interest backers who rely on the cheap labor. However it not just proves their phoniness in concern for civil liberties about the bill but shows their insincerity in fighting the war on terror.

Former Constitution Party candidate for president Chuck Baldwin in an article titled "Open Border Prove War On Terror is Superficial" stated that "for some seven years since the 9/11 attacks, our nation's borders and ports are as open and porous as ever. These open borders make the argument that "we are fighting them over there, so we won't have to fight them over here" look absolutely disingenuous—even laughable."

Baldwin adds "If the Bush administration was serious about fighting a war on terror, it would absolutely, resolutely, and immediately seal our borders and ports. It is nothing short of lunacy to send our National Guard forces to Iraq for the purpose of protecting that country's borders, while leaving America's borders wide open!"

There is legitimate concern about the bill leading to the arrest of American citizens but we are already in a police state with random searches and warrantless wiretaps. The Same individuals who are the biggest supporters of the police state are now outraged that it is

targeting illegal immigrants. This is because they are globalist who have

a vested interest in keeping our borders open.

# Netanyahu uses holocaust remembrance day to promote war with Iran

April 14, 2010

Israeli Prime Minister Benjamin used the holocaust memorial ceremony at Israel's Yav Vashem last Sunday to threaten Iran. The theme of his speech was that Iran is the new Nazi Germany and if Iran is not stopped there will be another holocaust. Netanyahu said "The historical failure of the free world in facing the Nazi beast was in not confronting it when it could still be stopped," Netanyahu said, "today we witness the fire of the old-new hate, the hate of the Jews being spread by the regimes and organizations of radical Islam, spearheaded by Iran and its cohorts."

Netanyahu added that "Iran's leaders are hell-bent on developing nuclear weapons and publicly declare their intention to destroy Israel, but in the face of the oft-repeated calls to erase the Jewish state from the face of the earth, we see at best mild protestations, and these too seem to be fading. "Netanyahu added that if "we do not hear the decisive condemnation required, the world stands by, some even criticize Israel. We do not see the international resolve required to prevent Iran's nuclear armament.

While Netanyahu did not directly threaten Iran he said "From this lectern I call on the enlightened nations to rise and powerfully condemn Iran's genocidal intentions and act with real resolve to stop Iran arming itself with nuclear weapons."

At the recent AIPAC convention Senator Lindsay Graham also used the holocaust to promote war with Iran, when he said "If you're a nation that wants to pursue nuclear power there should be an application, and if the president of that nation denies the existence of the Holocaust that should be the end of the application process."

He went on to call for a full out war saying "All options must be on the table. You know exactly what I'm talking about. The question is – do the people we're talking to understand what I'm talking about? I've been in the military as a support person. I've never been a combat troop walking down the streets of Iraq and Afghanistan, but I've been in the theater. I know that war is a terrible thing. It takes the lives of people at the prime of their life, and when you talk about war you should never talk about it with a smile on your face. But I do know this: that sometimes it's better to go to war than it is to allow the Holocaust to develop a second time.

In a recent interview Senator Joe Lieberman who is also demanding military action against Iran said that "the United States should begin preparing plans to attack Iran's nuclear program — and use that option if all diplomatic and other means fail." He added "I don't think it's time to use military force against Iran, but I certainly think it's time for the United States to have plans that will enable us to use force to stop the Iranian nuclear program if the president orders such an attack."

On the Amy Goodman Show former Israeli Minister Shulamit Aloni admitted that "When from Europe somebody is criticizing Israel then we bring up the holocaust. When in this country people are criticizing Israel then they are anti-Semitic. And the organization is strong and has a lot of money. And the ties between Israel and the American Jewish establishment are very strong and- they are strong in this country, as you know. And they have power, which is ok. They are talented people and they have power and money, and the media and other things, and their attitude is 'Israel my country right or wrong' , identification. And they are not ready to hear criticism. And it's very easy to blame people who criticize certain acts of the Israeli govt as anti-Semitic and to bring up the holocaust and the suffering of the Jewish people and that- that is justify everything we do to the Palestinians."

While Iranian regime is anti-Israel it is a flat out like to say that Ahmadinejad called for the destruction of Israel. Ahmadinejad never threatened to wipe Israel off the face of the map. These allegations come from a speech he gave at conference called a "World without Zionist", where he said the occupation regime over Jerusalem should vanish from the page of time." The world regime was misinterpreted for the nation of Israel. Ahmadinejad was not threatening Israel but that the

95

regime will inevitably collapse like those of the Shah of Iran and the Soviet Union. He said elections should be held among "Jews, Christians and Muslims so the population of Palestine can select their government and destiny for themselves in a democratic manner."

Netanyahu has refused to attend a meeting held by President Obama with 46 nations about how to keep nuclear weapons out of the hands of terrorist, due to the fact that Israel has long kept its nuclear arsenal a secret. However Netanyahu is outraged that the west isn't doing enough to stop Iran.

Iran knows that attacking Israel would be suicide but if Iran were able to achieve nuclear capabilities Israel would lose its geopolitical power as the soul Nuclear power in the middle east. Comparisons to the Nazis and the Holocaust are an effective way to stir up fear but is a gross distortion of the truth to say that Iran is the new Hitler since Israel has far superior military capabilities, hundreds of nukes, and the unconditional backing of the world number one superpower. Israel will probably not attack Iran itself anytime soon but they are using the threat of a lone attack to get western nations primarily the US to but greater pressure on Iran.

*The following are the only three written Robert Stark interviews ever published:*

# (1.) An Interview with Brett Stevens. -April 30th 2014

**[Robert Stark] 1. How has the rise of liberalism made an enemy out of Nationalism and Tradition?**

[Brett Stevens] In 1789, with the Revolution in France, the Western world split in two. There were those who favored the old way, which was based on the idea of a pervasive order of nature external to the human individual. And then there was the new group, who favored only the desires, feelings and judgments of human individuals.

We might call that older group realists, objectivists, conservatives, consequentialists or even simply "scientists." We might call the new group individualists, egomaniacs, narcissists or reality-deniers, but the fact remains that the new group are immensely more popular because they pander to the lowest common denominator impulses in all of us. We each wish, when we feel weak or sad, that our desires, feelings and judgments were more important than the complex and often baffling world around us.

Liberalism panders to this idea through its insistence on "equality," or the notion that whatever each person believes is more important than reality, including the limits of that person in any given situation. While the liberal idea is never stated in such plain terms, nor do liberals reveal how it develops quickly into its pure and extreme form, all liberal movements — communism, Democrats, progressivism, anarchism, leftism and socialism — are based in this singular idea of equality. As mentioned above, however, equality is shorthand for the human individual and its desires being more important than reality itself.

Liberals gain their power from their popularity, and so they specialize in removing any restrictions on the individual. As a result, they oppose any form of shared community values. This includes both nationalism, or the idea that a nation is defined by the common heritage, customs, language, culture and values of its citizens, and Tradition, or the idea that a transcendental order exists in nature and that humans find joy by understanding it instead of asserting our own desires, feelings and judgments against it.

In fact, since the French Revolution in 1789, liberalism has made "internationalism" or erasing of national borders, social classes and ethnic identities its primary goal. It gains its power from popularity, as mentioned above, so it specializes in turning the individual _against_ any form of culture. It goal is the creation of a lynch mob that votes against any form of power, wealth or intelligence higher than its own lowest common denominator. Seen in this light, liberalism is the perfect system of control because it is invisible to most people and yet controls all aspects of their lives. The only forces that oppose it are traditionalism, conservatism and nationalism, and those tend to be versions of the same idea.

## 2. How will these things save us from modernity?

Modernity is a type of civilization. It occurs only after liberalism has taken control. Because it tends to come later in the life-cycle of a civilization, it usually brings with it increases in wealth, technology and military power. However, what defines modernity is not the number of the year, but the way the civilization in which it arises is organized.

One way to view modernity is as a mid-life crisis. Civilization has grown up strong and youthful, conquered all the obstacles and climbed every mountain, and now it is less driven. It wants to go to bed earlier and wear comfortable but ludicrous slippers. Modernity is like a mid-life crisis: civilization has lost direction, and starts trying to please everyone at once. It "acts young" but can't even enjoy its old pleasures, so instead it tries to be popular by telling people what they want to hear.

Like most truly powerful crises, modernity does not announce itself this way. It portrays itself as youthful, altruistic, enlightened and compassionate. In reality, it is selfish and manipulative. 222 years after the French Revolution, our civilization is in ruins. We produce none of the quality art and culture of the past. Our "thinkers" are incapable of having competent or realistic thoughts. Our cities are ugly and we spend most of our lives waiting around for stupidity to end. Most of us hate our jobs, our commutes, and the constant blaring of commercial messages and the control that commerce has over every aspect of our society. Pulling back from our daily acceptance of this world, we can see that we live in hell.

Instead of good times, liberalism means social decay and the collapse of our civilization. It has brought us endless wars for Democracy and constant internal friction as our pluralist society tries to reconcile the fact that its citizens have no common ground with its dogma that demands that our common ground be a lack of common ground. It does all of this to smash any vestige of the old order, which is the startling notion that there is a world outside of the individual and that the rules of that world define what we should do.

Nationalism and Tradition will save us from modernity by opposing the one part of modernity that liberals try very hard to hide — its central principle. With liberalism, the central principle has two parts. The first is its public appearance, which is "equality" and the altruistic, pity and "progressive" politics that support it. The second part is not public. In fact, it's hidden. This part is the truth of equality, which is that it's an attempt to take control of this society by creating a huge mob of people who are easily controlled because they are trained to demand certain ideas, and smash anyone who has any other ideas.

Conservatism is the parent ideology of nationalism and tradition. Unlike liberalism, which focuses on what the individual wants to think, conservatism is based on a study of reality — in other words, what works. Conservatives are consequentialists, or those who study the results of our actions, and they believe that when we know all possible results, we can pick the results we want, and discipline our actions to match. This principle, along with nationalism and traditionalism, is the antithesis of liberalism.

If our civilization were to see even 2% of its population shift to an original sense of conservatism, including nationalism and traditionalism, that unified front would be active enough to create vast change. Liberalism fears that, which is why they do their best to demonize any true conservative movement by calling it racist, elitist, sexist or otherwise contrary to the values of 1789.

## 3. Explain how diversity itself rather than its ingredients is the problem with multiculturalism.

As part of the liberal agenda, it is essential to smash all shared community values and all culture in order to achieve total individual equality. One way liberals do this is to demand that societies become multicultural or "diverse," which are shorthand terms for racial, ethnic and cultural mixing. Liberals spin this to you as the idea that you'll have every possible variant of the human form ready for you to use, but in reality what happens is that all of these nifty cultures meld and create a singular cultureless gray race.

When multiculturalism appears, the temptation is for people of the majority group to criticize the minority groups that are now part of their lives. However, this misses the point. No matter what groups are chosen, the end result is the same (cultureless gray race). Even if the groups are similar, all shared culture is destroyed among each group, and what takes over is commerce, media and government propaganda. Throughout history, this has happened time and time again.

It doesn't take advanced technology to get to this stage. In fact, the ancient Romans and Greeks both experienced multiculturalism, thanks to their vast empires and their habit of bringing back new citizens to work doing basic labor (today's equivalents would be construction, food service and lawn care). The more multiculturalism came about, the less these ancient cultures were able to hold together, and finally they collapsed from within. It took multiple factors to bring them down, but multiculturalism was a big one, even though multiculturalism itself was a symptom of the decline. As any doctor can tell you, certain symptoms will kill you unless treated.

The problem with diversity is that by introducing many cultures into the same place, multiculturalism forces the adoption of a lowest common denominator. Since these cultures have little in common, and picking a culture will only offend other people, citizens invariably choose to have no culture except the innocuous stuff like television commercials, movies, celebrity gossip and fun facts about equality from government propaganda. The result is that since there is no common agreement on how to behave, people act selfishly and at random, which requires a strong police/nanny state to keep them in line.

If you want the proof of this, imagine an ethnic or religious group you're concerned about. Now, imagine them gone from the picture, but the multicultural state still existing. You may have to substitute other groups for them. In every combination, as long as there is a combination and not a single group, the result is the same. Whose holidays do we pick? Whose gods? Whose moral rules? Whose visual aesthetics and architecture? Whose music? The list goes on and on. Instead of a clear path and clear values system, you have chaos. And this is why the police state, oligarchs, and other "strongmen" come to power.

## 4. How come multi-culturalism takes the same form inevitably, no matter what we do?

Multiculturalism isn't defined by what it is, but by what it isn't. It is not a single culture. It is a mixture of cultures, which results by default in a non-culture. Just as two objects cannot occupy the same space at the same time, two or more cultures, religions, ethnic groups or races cannot occupy the same nation at the same time. The problem is not the specific differences, but the fact of difference itself. This is why every time multiculturalism has been tried, it has resulting in misery and decay. One metaphor is putting your food in a blender. If you take everything you were going to eat for dinner, dump it in a blender and turn it into a uniform mush, it's going to be disgusting, even if all of the individual parts were good. A quality steak, potato, salad and ice cream turns into vomitous goo. The problem is the blending, which multiculturalism forces, not the parts that are blended.

**5. How do you see the correlations between the fall of our modern civilization with the fall of empires thoughout history?**

The best way to visualize this, weirdly, is to compare it to a business. All businesses fail the same way. They get big and powerful and stop paying attention to the reality of the market and themselves. The result is that they either stop making products that people need, or become so disorganized and internally divided that they disintegrate even though they still have a lot to offer. This is a pattern that we see repeated time and time again. There's a similar pattern for societies, and it is basically the same idea: get big, stop paying attention to reality, become internally divided and then fall apart.

We have this myth in our modern time that we are immune to collapse because we have all this technology and wealth. However, the Romans and Greeks had much more technology and wealth than their neighbors, too. They were the most powerful civilizations of those days. They also found out that "too big to fail" is an illusion. They stopped paying attention to reality, lost track of the values they had in common, and as a result became more oppressive states that tried to use power to keep people in line, since culture had failed. At that point, their citizens became individualistic and decadent and displayed the values and behaviors that liberals today also share. Multiculturalism wracked their cities, as did hedonism and perversity. As a result, they fell apart from within.

The most interesting part is that this pattern applies to empires outside the West as well. Jared Diamond, who normally writes leftist propaganda, took a break to write a study of the civilization on Easter Island and how it fell apart from within. In the New World, the ancient Maya, Inca and Aztecs showed the exact same pattern, which left their civilizations weak and near death by the time the Spanish arrived to crudely finish the job. Even ancient Asian and African civilizations, from Angkor Wat to Egypt, showed this pattern of decline.

As with multiculturalism, societal collapse does not involve a bad guy we can isolate and smash. There is no tangible enemy. The enemy is disorder, and the lack of social order is what causes the decline, just as the fact of mixing destroys culture and thus causes the destruction that accompanies multiculturalism. The message of history is clear: you either hold your civilization together by having the same identity, culture, language, customs and values, or you fall apart.

What is interesting is how many works of ancient cultures deal with this theme. The epic of Gilgamesh touches on it; the Bhagavad-Gita is almost exclusively about it. The cornerstone of Western philosophy, Plato's "Republic," is written on this topic. Across the globe and throughout history, the problem of collapse and decline has fascinated and horrified our best thinkers, and they have come up with similar solutions — but all acknowledge that once we make popularity of an idea more important than its veracity, societies are unlikely to elect to choose those solutions.

## 6. What can we do to delay this process?

Surprisingly, the answer is simple but it may require some complicated methods. I'll break it down into three sections:

(1) Re-assert culture. Culture is organic and arises from the people, so it's hard to resurrect once it's gone. However, you can start with the older works of the past, and by going back to folk common sense, folk values and customs, and any traditions we can read about or learn from our elders. Make culture the dominant part of our lives. Instead of asking "What do I want to do today?" ask yourself "What is the activity that feels 'right' in light of what I know about our customs, calendar and values?" For this to take hold, it needs to be instilled in the public. One way to start this is to throw out all "art" from after our cultural decline. Get rid of the bad books, weird modern art, and mindless two-note pop music. Replace it with the greatness of the past and, once we learn how it works, with our own contributions.

(2) End the reign of popularity. Trends define us now and rule us. When something is popular, all of our merchants rush to it in order to cash in. Then there's a huge crowd of people with no direction in life — normally called "liberals" — and they rush toward the trends because each one of them wants a chance to be important and to share in the drama. Then government and media pay attention. Soon it's a giant cycle of a huge in-group deciding that some idea is "important" and then selling it to each other. We can retaliate against this by putting some limits on consumerism, including cheap products from abroad; restricting the vote

106

to people age 30+ who own homes; taxing mass media as if it were shipping a physical product; and perhaps most importantly, visibly dropping out of the rush for popularity. We need to refute it in all of its forms. All of this starts with us making fun of it, mocking the people who are addicted to it, and refusing to participate not on political grounds but on practical grounds like "Television bores me" and "Celebrities are too neurotic for me." Finally, I think we should encourage software, news, video game, movie and audio piracy in order to sabotage and destroy our media industry.

## 7. Is there a way to rebuild it after it happens?

Civilizations have been destroyed and rebuilt many times before. What happens is that about ten percent of the population, generally not survivalist types and not social butterflies either, decide to carry on their culture, technology and people and start up somewhere else. In fact, the classic epic poem "Aeneid" by Virgil conveys this very theme. Aeneas of Troy and his cohorts have fled the scene of their vast loss in battle and have evaded the victorious Greeks and set sail for a new homeland, where it is foretold that Aeneas will found a new and great civilization. The Aeneid is quite a stirring writing based on many historical sources, but what's most important is that it accurately describes the process by which people rebuild.

What is different in our case is that we do not want to abandon Europe or America; we want to rebuild them. This presents a quandary because our cities are choked with people, most of whom have no useful skills.

What will most likely occur is, as has happened in the distant past, our strongest people will withdraw to less-populated and un-trendy areas, where they will build centers of great wealth and power. They will then slowly reconquest the other land, probably by becoming enough of a threat to the interlopers there that those interlopers will flee, leaving behind the land. What civilization rebuilders need is (a) knowledge, (b) quality people and (c) land. It doesn't matter if we cannot recapture New York or L.A. — any open patch of land with access to lake or ocean will do. When the rebuilt civilization becomes more powerful or more numerous than the remnants of the ruined culture that came before it, the new civilization will conquer the old and exile its people, and then be in complete control.

**8. Why does liberalism always target the "favored" in order to promote its agenda, equality though distribution of wealth and crippling of ability?**

If you want equality, you have two options for achieving it: either you try to raise up the lesser, or bring down the greater. Raising the lesser doesn't really work, because if someone is in a lesser position it is usually because they have screwed up and/or lack abilities needed to rise above that level. This leaves bringing down the stronger, which is easier to do. As in the Kurt Vonnegut story "Harrison Bergeron," you just handicap the more competent people so that they are only barely able to compete with the incompetents around them. This brings everybody down to the same level.

108

Interestingly, modern liberalism uses both methods. It creates a massive welfare state for those who are not succeeding like the poor, incompetents, gays/lesbians/bisexuals/transsexuals, minorities, women, the obese, mental health cases. At the same time, it tries to bury its most intelligent and capable people in a mountain of red tape, regulations, unstable cities and pointless governmental exercises. Affirmative action, the welfare state, and high schools that bore intelligent children are all part of this liberal method.

## 9. How would you solve the issues of wealth distribution such as the concentration of wealth and power among a tiny few?

I wouldn't. This problem is a non-issue that solves itself. The Paris Hiltons of the world will manage to waste their money and new people will take their places. What is most important is having a society where the competent and motivated people can rise above the rest. This method, which when it occurs in nature we call "natural selection" or "Darwinian evolution," simply works because it means that the people on top are GENERALLY the most productive, intelligent, moral and hard-working types. Everyone benefits from having the most capable people at the top, even if it means those capable people become quite wealthy.

If you are a Christian, you can see this expressed in the parable of the talents. A master leaves money with his three servants; one buries the coins, and gives back the exact same coins; another invests the coins and has mediocre performance, but is able to return the same amount;

109

the third invests the money well, makes a lot more, and returns that. If you're the master, you're going to take a much bigger sum of money and give it to the servant who can invest it well and make more of it. That way, everybody wins. There is more money for everyone.

While the "libertarians" we see floating around are often not the best examples, I like the basic principle of libertarianism. Get the regulation out of the way and let the best people rise. This encourages every citizen to think not in terms of what they deserve, or how they're victims, but in terms of what they can do to make more wealth. It's a healthier mental state than waiting around for government handouts or pity.

**10. A. Do you think that Capitalism is worth preserving or should we look to some third way economic theory such as distributism?**

My answer here is classic New Right: capitalism is the best possible economic system, if and only if we keep it under the thumb of culture. We need to have shared values that come first, and then capitalism should serve that. Without culture to rein it in, capitalism becomes a voracious parasite that tears a society apart. Of course, without culture, any aspect of a society becomes parasitic because they are all running out of control without leadership.

**B. Should we oppose big business and big finance as we do to big government?**

The entire reason I'm a nationalist is to avoid "opposing" institutions that are required as a result of our social order. In America as it is currently

110

designed, we have a huge mass of grey culture proles who need a giant nanny/police state to keep herd over them. Because they have nothing in common, they can be counted on to do random destructive acts when not constantly watched over, and to randomly cause conflicts with each other. To try to ride herd on this vast morass of confused citizenry, we have welfare agencies, help groups, police forces, counselors, disciplinarians, and millions of bureaucrats. In addition, big business exists because the more clueless the population gets, the more services they need just to make it through the day. When you think about it, America as a frontier nation did not have big government or big companies, and not just because such things did not exist — they were known in Europe. However, there was no need. Everyone knew what the task was and had a role in it. The same thing is true of the healthy nations in Europe. Everyone joins hands because they perceive a common values system, goal, culture, heritage, identity and history, and there's a far lesser need for enforcement of any kind, and certainly not for a nanny state. We have a government that seems to spend most of its time trying to save idiots from themselves. Our corporations spend their time designing entertainment and convenience products for vast herds of sofa-bound citizens. Do we need this? We would not, if we had a nationalist and tradition society created with paleoconservative principles. Culture would guide us, and shape the role of both government and citizen. A self-help mentality would pervade the population, and the loss of stupid people through accident would not be a "tragedy" but a normal event. The result would be a self-maintaining, healthier society that would not need the nanny state or its commercial lapdogs.

**11. Explain how liberalism, egalitarianism, and anti-elitism share a common root in human psychology.**

The root of liberalism is fear. The individual fears that they are not capable. For that reason, they start to hate and resent those who are having a good time in life. At that point, the situation becomes sort of like the plot of a Hollywood movie — think of Napoleon Dynamite: the nerdy kids join together, form a little mob, and take on the rich, good-looking and powerful kids, and win. The crowd takes over. The outcasts triumph over the successes. Everything is reversed and inverted. This is the common root of all liberalism, egalitarianism and anti-elitism. They exist because of the fear of individuals. Those individuals find a way to gain power, which is to concoct this absurd fiction of "equality" and use it to force their way into power. What is always popular, especially among those who are less capable? Equality — it means that even if you contribute nothing, you're guaranteed a place at the table. Who has no use for equality? Those who have risen above it. And so that's who the liberals target. All of this originates in a root in human psychology, which is our tendency to project our fear onto the world and by making parts of that world symbols of our fear and smashing them, to think we have escaped our fear.

**12. Explain how they form the basis of decay.**

112

Once liberalism appears in your civilization, each of your citizens is a free agent. They are no longer bonded toward a common goal and values system, like culture. They are acting for themselves, selfishly, and against the rest of society, which they see as "oppressing" them. Even more, suddenly all of your citizens want to act like victims and have someone else do the work and make the hard choices. Their agenda becomes the classic liberal agenda not of generating wealth and power, but of redistributing wealth and creating democracy. At that point, decay is gaining strength because the society has lost any sight of reality itself.

## 13. A. Do you defend elitism?

Absolutely I defend elitism. However, I need to separate elitism from its cousin, pretense. Elitism means that you pick the best possible option and push yourself to the highest possible goals. That's it. Pretense works the opposite way, which is that you assume you are important, and in order to justify that appearance, you start claiming that the stuff you like is of the highest quality and everyone else should respect it. Elitism is the enemy of pretense because elitism demands actual performance. If you're going shopping for music, buy the best. If you're in school, all praise goes to the smart kids and best athletes. If you're doing a job, you hold yourself to high standards. Pretense is when people pick something obscure and claim it's the best possible thing, and they do this for one reason and one reason only, which is that it gives them more control and more social power over you.

**B. If the ideas of the left such as egalitarianism are anti-elitist explain why the entire elite of the west supports them?**

Elitism means support of the best. That scares our western liberals, so they have constructed false elites. Just as natural selection scares them, so they created equality, they are now creating false reasons to be "elite" such as having politically correct opinions, being socially popular and being inoffensive. This does not qualify anyone as an elitist. In fact, you can ONLY be a liberal elitist if you are egalitarian, which is the opposite of being an elitist (it's like being a vegetarian carnivore). Egalitarianism is the opposite of elitism which is why our (false) "elites" will not accept anyone who is not egalitarian.

**C. We have discussed how egalitarianism reduces human output to the lowest common demoninator. what is your take on populism and especially how it relates to elitism?**

The left uses the term "populism" to refer to any right-wing movement with popular support, but a more sensible definition is pandering to the immediate financial and social demands of a population. If done at the expense of long-term plans, this is very destructive, but otherwise, it's important to realize that a nation like an army runs on its stomachs. Political leaders need to make sure that the demands for dogma do not outweigh the need for people to have stable lives, income, food and medical care (and the like). Our current president has put much of that stuff on the back burner in order to work on ideological objectives, and Soviet-style infrastructure failure has resulted from it.

## 14. How come the environmental movement is deeply confused?

When you introduce liberalism into a movement, no other goals are possible. Liberalism is a binary movement: you are either liberal, or you are the enemy of liberalism. That is because liberalism is its own agenda and all of the issues that liberals like are means to that end. Multiculturalism? Smash the majority, create equality. Drug use? Smash morality, create equality. Atheism? Smash religion, create equality. Sodomy? Smash normalcy, create equality. Their goal is to make every choice, idea, decision, preference, person and concept "equal" so that no choice is more valuable than any other. This means every individual will feel accepted, and anyone who creates a value shared between people will be viewed with suspicion.

Obviously, this outlook doesn't play well with others! It's very hostile, inherently defensive and views itself as a victim, and as such is highly reactionary and aggressive. It's like a cancer. The environmental movement allowed itself to be swallowed up by liberalism sometime in the 1950s. This meant that instead of simply working toward a better environment, the environmental movement was working toward a better environment — through liberalism. As a result, environmentalists stopped talking about conserving the forests and started talking about how equality and multiculturalism will save our forests. Not surprisingly, at that point every sane person tuned out, because it was like listening to Soviet Radio to hear these people talk.

Right now, environmentalists refuse to talk about the actual problems of nature and the solutions. Instead you get lots of expensive lightbulbs filled with mercury, people telling you to stop whaling and start recycling your condoms, and toilets that take two flushes instead of one. What are liberal-environmentalists avoiding? Population, for one. We've got seven billion people and the next stop is nine billion. Next, most of these people are impoverished and having lots of kids. They're also avoiding what happens when we try to give all nine billion of these people a first-world lifestyle, with fast food and two cars and a house. Further, they're not mentioning the big problem, which is use of land. For every 100 sq ft we live in, there's probably another 10,000 sq ft of land for farms, roads, hospitals, schools, parking lots, airports, warehouses, stores, restaurants, bars, and government buildings.

What nature really needs is conservation. However, environmentalists will not accept that. Conservation is a right-wing movement that involves setting aside land for nature. As a result, conservation means we stop telling everyone that they're entitled to a house, car, wealthy lifestyle, etc. just because they are human and therefore equal. Instead, we work toward having fewer humans by putting a lot of the land off-limits and letting natural species thrive. By off-limits, we mean no roads, no fences, no power lines and no "guaranteed safety." We mean keeping the land wild and if you get eaten by a bear or wander three miles off a trail and fall to your death, oh well. That's part of nature, the un-cuddly and scary parts. The bigger point is that for us to have the many species of plants and animal out there, we need to give them space to hunt, play, mate and rear young. They need more space than we think. We can't put them in zoo-cage-sized plots and hope they'll thrive. But all of that is not acceptable to environmentalists, who are liberals first and environmental activists a distant second.

### 15. Explain your ideology of deep ecology?

Let me first quote from the Deep Ecology Movement's mission statement:

"We believe that true ecological sustainability may require a rethinking of our values as a society. Present assumptions about economics, development, and the place of human beings in the natural order must be reevaluated. If we are to achieve ecological sustainability, Nature can no longer be viewed only as a commodity; it must be seen as a partner and model in all human enterprise.

We begin with the premise that life on Earth has entered its most precarious phase in history. We speak of threats not only to human life, but to the lives of all species of plants and animals, as well as the health and continued viability of the biosphere. It is the awareness of the present condition that primarily motivates our activities.

We believe that current problems are largely rooted in the following circumstances:

* The loss of traditional knowledge, values, and ethics of behavior that celebrate the intrinsic value and sacredness of the natural world and

that give the preservation of Nature prime importance. Correspondingly, the assumption of human superiority to other life forms, as if we were granted royalty status over Nature; the idea that Nature is mainly here to serve human will and purpose.

* The prevailing economic and development paradigms of the modern world, which place primary importance on the values of the market, not on Nature. The conversion of nature to commodity form, the emphasis upon economic growth as a panacea, the industrialization of all activity, from forestry to farming to fishing, even to education and culture; the drive to economic globalization, cultural homogenization, commodity accumulation, urbanization, and human alienation. All of these are fundamentally incompatible with ecological or biological sustainability on a finite Earth.

* Technology worship and an unlimited faith in the virtues of science; the modern paradigm that technological development is inevitable, invariably good, and to be equated with progress and human destiny. From this, we are left dangerously uncritical, blind to profound problems that technology and science have wrought, and in a state of passivity that confounds democracy.

* Overpopulation, in both the overdeveloped and the underdeveloped worlds, placing unsustainable burdens upon biodiversity and the human condition.

As our name suggests, we are influenced by the Deep Ecology Platform, which helps guide and inform our work. We believe that values other than market values must be recognized and given importance, and that Nature provides the ultimate measure by which to judge human endeavors." (http://www.deepecology.org/mission.htm)

If you read this statement carefully, you see that what it calls for is a role best filled by a traditional society. We need values outside of commerce, trends and popularity; this means we need culture. We need sanctity of the natural world as part of those values, which means we need a traditional outlook on society and religion. We need smaller civilizations more closely bonded to the land, which is nationalism. The National Socialist Germans talked about "Blood and Soil," but they picked that phrase up from the Volkisch movement, which was also the parent of the original German environmental movement. We need strong culture, national identity and strong pro-nature values in order to want to do what is right (i.e. difficult) to preserve our environment.

**16. Why do you think the right wants nothing to do with environmentalism?**

Once the left took over environmentalism, the right fled it. The media is not liberal-controlled, but it's leftist-sympathetic because over 75% of the people who work in media are leftist, and the media overlords know that liberalism is more popular than conservatism so they pander to liberal values. As a result, what a normal person saw was that environmentalism meant socialism with a tacked-on afterthought saying

119

"Oh yeah, and help the animals and plants too, when we're done with the wealth redistribution." This caused the right to get the heck away from environmentalism, because the environmentalist movement was basically a liberal recruiting ground.

**17. You also state that you see modern environmentalism focusing too much on trivial issues. Give examples and what are the more serious issues they should focus on?**

(This was probably answered in #14)

**18. Is a significant degree of government intervention necessary to preserve the environment?**

In a traditional society, culture is more important than government. As a result, government serves culture. The opposite is true in our time, where government serves itself and uses liberal talking points to justify itself. In a truly traditional society, agreement among the leaders both official and unofficial would be in favor of radical conservationism. These leaders would be clergy, business leaders, teachers, police, firefighters, academics, small business owners and military people — normal people, but people who had proven their ability to lead. They would influence others. If our architecture emphasized buildings set apart from each other by wide-open unbroken natural spaces, and our social values emphasized huge forests where no one went, and all of our television programs praised the wild frontier, we'd have our results without government having to do anything.

## 19. What is green conservatism?

Green conservatism is the idea that conservatives conserve, and we conserve the environment too. Currently, the right-wing is in a bad state because fundamental right-wing values like social Darwinism, elitism, natural selection, nationalism, shared values (but not collective force), and strong culture are forbidden and classified as taboo by the liberal majority. To avoid being banned, right-wing parties hide their true nature and make themselves hybrids with liberalism, which gets us neo-conservatism. Neo-conservatism will not embrace environmentalism because it is too infected with the leftist agenda, but also because neo-conservatism is too infected with liberal dogma. As a result, the right is distanced from greenism. However, it makes sense for us to re-adopt this value and take it back from the left. We believe in nature and in the natural order, and it's sensible for the right-wing to come up with a conservative platform for environmentalism and green activism, which is outlined above in the "deep ecology" and conservation questions.

## 20. How it would it be implemented and what are some positions it would take to preserve the environment?

(This was probably answered in #14)

## 21. Explain what is futurist traditionalism.

Futurist traditionalism is conservatism without the dead parts. We want to learn from the past and apply those lessons toward having a better future. We recognize that every society needs a clear identity, shared values, heritage, culture, language and customs in order to thrive. We want a rising society, or one that isn't so obsessed with wealth redistribution that it forgets to do great things. We want an end to idiocracy, which is a product of egalitarianism, and an end to liberal democracy. Instead, we want a society that can assert its values and act toward realizing them. This requires we keep the traditionalist nature of all successful societies to date, and introduce futurism, or a desire to reach toward the future through technology and learning. We want to discard what conservatism has become, which is defensive and boring, and replace it with a desire to conquer the universe and to be better than we thought we could be. We desire greatness, beauty and adventure. We're not stodgy old reactionaries like the liberals, who are still spouting the lies from 1789 and trying to use guilt to control us.

**22. Explain how conservatism is about learning from the past and nature.**

Conservatism is based on understanding cause/effect relationships. History is our laboratory, and we hope to learn from our mistakes. When we see how a certain cause ended up, we know whether we want to repeat it or avoid it. This is analogous to how natural selection works in nature, where good ideas result in success and bad ideas result in failure. Even more, nature teaches us that all good designs come with an inherent beauty and grace that not only is functional, but makes us feel at home and in awe of our universe. Paul Woodruff wrote a great book about this called "Reverence."

122

### 23. Why don't modern conservatives respect the past and nature?

Modern conservatives are neoconservatives, or half-liberal/half-conservative hybrids. Like most hybrids, they have some "hybrid vigor" in that they are driven forward by the contradictions in their ideology, but over time it starts to break apart. Among the modern conservatives are many paleoconservatives, who hold on to the older and truer conservatism of people like H.L. Mencken and T.S. Eliot and before. These respect the past and nature. Modern conservatives cannot respect the past and nature because it clashes with the values they have adopted from liberalism. The past was not egalitarian, and yet society was better — as a result, it's politically incorrect and social taboo to mention the past. Nature rewards the competent, which is against equality as well.

### 24. Explain the existentialist case for conservatism.

Life should be beautiful and exciting, filled with discovery and adventure, and giving each individual a sense of place and purpose. You cannot do that by telling everyone they must be equal and that they can do whatever they want that does not offend others. What that translates into is a society of single people alone in their apartments for the eight hours a day they're not at jobs, pursuing their hobbies alone because otherwise they might cause someone to be upset. Freedom, equality and "peace" sound good on paper but in reality they're a form of entropy. Nothing changes; everything is a surface appearance with no depth. The conservatives of the future are the people who are bored with modern society because it is adventureless, ugly and without a goal. These people want a challenge and want a beautiful life, not just a utilitarian one. That is how existentialist sentiments direct people toward conservatism.

**25. Explain how the ensuing social chaos demands a strong force of control, found in commerce, media and government.**

When we have a strong culture or shared values system (including actual "common sense") people do what is sensible according to that values system. Since everyone shares this values system it is easy to know what you should be doing and what you should avoid. As a result, the only deviants are criminals, and those are dealt (preferably by exile).

Without that values system, people have no idea what they should be doing. In addition, equality means they are faceless and anonymous, so they start "acting out" in an attempt to stand out from the crowd and be recognized socially. This means that sheer chaos reigns. Every individual is doing something different, usually without purpose, and since they desire "different" more than "logical," they end up creating mayhem wherever they go. The ensuing social breakdown requires a strong police state to keep deviancy in line when it goes far; in addition, government and media collude to preach simple commands at the people to keep them from screwing up. For example, look at the massive campaigns against cigarettes, drugs, DUI, incest, child abuse, etc. that so elegantly line our freeways and fill our magazines. That's propaganda. We don't object because we think it's a good cause. But when your society has so few values in common that you have to educate people to not rape their children, we're past the point where good causes can help anything.

**26. While mainstream conservatives focus on how people are dependent on the government you also focus on how they are too dependent on entertainment and social approval. Explain?**

Without culture, people are looking for meaning in their lives. Since there's no goal in common to work toward, all that is left is ourselves — who we are as social constructions, who we know and what kind of personal drama we have going on at the moment. This makes social approval become important. In fact, it becomes the only way they measure themselves. Liberalism encourages this, because liberalism is fundamentally a social movement, or a fashion, or trend.

All of these social ideas cause people to stop thinking about real goals. Instead of trying to achieve something, they ask "How will this look to others?" Instead of having real values, they wonder "Will this make other people like me?" And instead of acting with purpose, they look for novelty and distraction, so that other people find it interesting.

The media plays into this both as a provider of memes, and as a parasite that follows trends and hypes them up so that each group can get its turn. The coolfinders come first, the hipsters imitate them, then middle America imitates that, and then the true drop-outs get a turn. It's just like trendy products, like those dumb plastic singing fish. At first, they're rare and kind of hip and a few people own them. Then, Target gets ahold of it and sells it to middle class America. Finally, at some point down the line, K-mart and Wal-mart start selling the things in bulk at a discount, but at that point only the hopelessly un-hip buy them. It's like a giant ecosystem where the media stimulates trends, then markets products for them.

As a consequence of this, most of modern society lives in a place that doesn't resemble reality at all. We had millions of people worldwide convinced that Troy Davis was innocent because that's what CNN said and that's what all their friends said. If they had the police file in front of them and read it, they would have been thinking, "Wait just a second — this guy is not a good person, he's guilty as hell." But instead they let the social trends, media memes and popular fashion sway their thinking. It's how crowds are dangerous.

### 27. Explain how America is a type of civilization rather than a place.

There's a lot of hatred for America in the world, and 99% of it is caused by (a) envy or (b) distrust of American policies. I don't hate America, and don't see the point; the real issue is that modern society is the source of those American policies many of us distrust. America is a civilization in its modern stage, which is a kind of mid-life crisis. What makes America seem so horrible to people is that we are caught in a liberal time, and so we are preaching liberalism to the world, yet as our society decays it

126

becomes apparent that our "gift" of liberal democracy is anything but a gift — it's a death sentence.

Instead of hating America, the smart people out there should realize that America is a country like any other, and the disease that grips America can grip other countries too. America is just ahead of the game because it never had as clear of an ethnic consensus, and because as a rapidly growing highly social civilization, it has surged ahead to encounter these challenges. What has happened to America can happen to any country, however, and indeed has happened to all empires before they have fallen.

**28. Comprised of equal parts liberal anarchism and commercial fascism, this type of civilization uses "freedom" and "equality" to create a society without standards, values or ideals — what does this mean?**

Our society endorses liberal values, which at their fullest expression take form in anarchy: everyone is equal, no one rises above to make rules. At the same time, an anarchist society would rapidly develop commerce and armed security guards because as long as there are people, there will be a need for services and a vast profit potential. Any society that did away with money and government would find itself in short order in the grips of far more powerful forces of commerce and a police state. Our society gets as close to the anarchist ideal as it can and also tries to keep its citizens happy with commerce, so it ends up creating a balance by which the citizens do whatever they want so long

127

as they do not intrude on the commerce. This is a problem because without culture to guide it, commerce becomes parasitic and destructive. However, both commerce and anarchistic liberalism agree on one thing — no rules, except the obvious protection of commerce, no murder, etc. This means such as society is violently opposed to standards, values and ideals because these conflict with the absolute equality of anarchism and the absolute corrupting force of commerce.

**29. The ensuing social chaos demands a strong force of control, found in commerce, media and government. Commerce ropes citizens into debt and jobs, media fills their heads with illusions, and government enforces profitable laws — what does this mean?**

When you do away with standards in common, you introduce social chaos. Our government has no interest in limiting that chaos because it provides a justification for its power. In the meantime, people are tired of it, so they flock to commercial messages and products which promise peace, relaxation, etc. No one wants to admit that our cities are ugly, our people are chaotic, and as a result our civilization is disorganized, boring, and fundamentally soulless.

**30. You believe that peaceful revolution can occur if 5% of the population adopts your ideas?**

5% would be nice but even 2% of the population, if they give up on their "individualism" and join together toward a goal in common, can effect a massive change in the world. All it takes is consistency and dedication.

All revolutions start this way. It's easier for liberal revolutions, because their ideas are popular, but as liberalism fails more people are turning toward the new forms of conservatism.

## 31. Explain how immigration is class warfare and causes racism.

Immigration is a tool of the liberal left. It is used to destroy the majority by forcing a new culture into our country, thus putting the former majority culture on the defensive, with any incidents of friction used to induce guilt in members of that majority culture. Further, it imports a huge number of new liberal voters. The ultimate goal is to shatter culture, destroy values consensus and replace members of the majority with impoverished newcomers; in addition, the influx displaces lower income Americans from their jobs and forces them either into poverty or into jobs for which they may not be qualified. The result is fear and trembling all around, but the ultimate goal is class warfare against the wealthy majority and the replacement of that majority with a new population.

## 32. Explain how immigration is fundamentally racist since it seeks to destroy a race and replace it with a new one.

Immigration is multiculturalism, unless we're talking about immigration from Europe. America is a European nation by how her founding fathers saw her and by the dominant Anglo-Germanic culture of the time. It was only in the 1840s that we opened America up to non-Northwestern Europeans, and only in the 1960s that we opened it up to non-European descended people. The result has been replacement of a vague but vital original culture with the culture of not having a culture, or multiculturalism. The goal of multiculturalism is not to provide us with more exciting ethnic foods, but to replace us. The new people will be more likely to vote liberal. They will also take their revenge on those they are certain have oppressed them.

**33. You reviewed Jared Taylor's new book. Explain your take on it.**

Jared Taylor wrote a real masterpiece with "White Identity: Racial Consciousness in the 21st Century." Over the past 40 years, we've learned a lot about diversity. The problem is not African-Americans, Jews, Hispanics, Asians, etc. but the fact of diversity itself, which both (a) destroys our shared values and identity and (b) replaces those with a culture dedicated to having no values. Diversity is conformity. We don't recognize it as conformity because it is spun to us as an "alternative" to a ("boring") ethnic majority, and we're told by our televisions that we are boring and have no culture, so we must import some. However, the end result of diversity is uniformity in a mixed-ethnic, cultureless void. Taylor starts out his book by recognizing the value of ethnic identity and the shared cultural values it brings. He discusses this first in other ethnic groups, and then in white people. Then, without falling back into criticism of the ingredients of diversity, he explores recent research that shows us how destabilizing and sabotaging diversity is. As Taylor notes, this diversity does not have to be racial or ethnic, as even same-race and same-ethnic groups have disintegrated under diverse conditions if separated by religion, philosophy or even radical gaps in social class. He points out the role of diversity in destroying aging civilizations. It's a compelling argument, diligently researched, and written very well. I highly recommend this book and Pat Buchanan's "Suicide of a Superpower." If you read them together, you see the whole picture at once.

**34. With the state of modern conservativism, what makes you want to hold on to that label rather than go in some other direction such as third position?**

I used to like the idea of third positionism, but then I reconsidered history. All of history until 1789 showed us a solid conservative underpinning to society that while it had its problems, was nothing like the chaos and crass mundane evil that seems to define modern society. For that reason, I do not see a reason for a third position; conservatism is the sane position, and liberalism is a product of decay. You don't try to find reasons to argue around decay. In addition, we already have a third position, which is pre-1789 conservatism with its caste system, monarchies, traditions, and highly ritualized daily experience. The last thing I want to do is create a path because it seems socially acceptable and like it might attract people who are afraid of conservatism. I think instead it makes sense to explain that the right is correct and always has been, and that we can find solutions to all of our modern problems by simply avoiding all liberalism. Liberalism destroys civilization. That which is not liberalism, and is realistic and common sense, is conservatism. I want to re-make conservatism so it's more like the

Traditionalist movement, the pale-conservatives, and so that it recaptures its deep ecologist conservationist roots. But I see no reason to abandon it. Its appeal is that it is a collection of strategies for living that simply work. Its triumph over liberalism is that liberalism is airy theory that sounds good to your friends, but doesn't work. As year 222 rolls past and Europe's and America's fortunes remain in a screaming downward spiral, more and more people are realizing that we went wrong in 1789 and the solution is not to invent some new method, but to simply stop making the bad choice to perpetuate liberalism. We took a wrong turn; we need to retrace our steps, fix the damage, pick ourselves up and move on.

### 35. Is a new political party necessary to implement your ideas?

This sounds flippant, but no, I'd rather implement them directly. We have an entirely workable conservative establishment in which it is not a mystery that diversity doesn't work, that the entitlement state is death, and that liberalism destroys the family and produces alienated cultureless citizens — heck, these things aren't a mystery on the left, either, but they're planning to use these social disruptions (Alinsky was not the first to think of this) to seize power permanently and destroy the majority so no challenge to their power remains. If normal citizens start rising in the Republican ranks and demanding polite and logical attention to these issues, change will occur.

### 36. What were the aims of the Frankfurt school how haw sucessful were they at implementing their ideas?

132

Let's backtrack through history. 1789 was the first open liberal revolt in the West; before that, stirrings had existed but mainly confined themselves to religion. The Frankfurt School came about at a time when liberals were first realizing the power of internationalism and the starry-eyed progressive appeal, and so certain academics decided to subvert traditional concepts through "theory" (where I'm from, theories are supposed to be about reality, not airy constructions removed from any workable notion of reality). This was part of the same political struggle, internationalism versus nationalism, that formed the basis of the two world wars. After the fall of the Soviet Union in the early 1990s, the Frankfurt School took on a new direction — merge Marxism with consumerism. I see the Frankfurt School as a subset of the European pro-anarchist/socialist drive of the 1910s and 1920s. It's useful to note that whether it calls itself leftism, liberalism, internationalism, globalism, anarchism, socialism, liberal democracy or communism, it's all the same ideology, just separated by small matters of degree.

**37. What is the driving ideological force behind our foreign policy in the mideast. Some say its humanitarian interventionism, American hegemenomny, the millitary industrial complex, Israeli interest?**

I think it's building our own image of ourselves. We have to show our citizens that we are right, and we are bringing a better world order through liberalism, so we need to (a) fight wars for democracy and (b) open up these new places to our business to destroy their culture and

133

enrich ourselves with their raw material wealth. Like all good liberal plans, this one relies on an altruistic public truth that conceals a private self-interested motivation. It just happens to dovetail, quite frequently, with what we need to do as a superpower. For example, the big powers now are Russia, China and India against the USA. It's sensible to knock out any potential allies. This is why the US is all over Eastern Europe and trying to infiltrate it with our business as quickly as possible. If we own those assets, the Russians and Chinese don't. So far India has played it smart and stayed friendly with the US and neutral to the Soviet Union while committing to neither. The sad truth of this situation is that US foreign policy generally produces good results. Any time a first-world society conquers a third-world society, that third-world society inherits many benefits of the first-world experience and eventually is incorporated into the first world empire. It's what the Romans did and Greeks did, and now it's what we do.

Regarding Israel, since that's what a lot of people are curious about when they ask about the middle east, I think it's important to realize that there are many groups competing for our political power and they all do it the same way — by getting dollars into the hands of lobbyists. We now have a huge pro-shariah lobby in this country and a huge liberal establishment that is if not outright anti-Semitic at the very least anti-Israel, who they accuse of apartheid (that's liberal slang for "ethnic self-preservation," apparently). There's also a huge fundamentalist Christian lobby with a hilarious forked tongue: they're pro-Israel, but only so that the final battle can occur at Har-Megiddo and we can all go up to the sky in The Rapture. To me, it seems obvious the Jews in Israel are fighting the same struggle that white people in Europe and the USA are, which is self-preservation against a third-world horde that is attempting to use our egalitarian philosophy to force us to accept them. They are aided by huge liberal camps in all three areas. Remove the liberals, and the problem goes away. It is probably in everyone's interest to have Israel rule the middle east — the Israeli average IQ is one standard deviation above the next best comer in the region. Israelis are simply smarter, on average, and we should probably let them positively influence the area. That's not to say the game couldn't change tomorrow — if the Arab league decides to suddenly exterminate all of its own citizens under 120 IQ points, Israel would face a smarter enemy that still outnumbered them. But that's a really hard strategy for any leader to take.

**38. I noticed you follow some of the manosphere blogs. What is your take on the trends in regards to relations between the sexes and the sociosexual marketplace? Ironically the traditional system of monogamy was much more egalitarian while the sexual revolution that the left has cheered on has led to a much less egalitarian sexual marketplace.**

Our society is falling apart, and the family has been disintegrating at a rapid rate since 1968. The result is that few people have any concept of love, but they're all good with the idea of sexual convenience, which serves the needs of the state and commerce. Was monogamy more egalitarian? It forced men to demonstrate some value before entering into a sexual contract. The sexual revolution has put women at a massive disadvantage by reducing their value and forcing them to endure much more misery before they achieve any permanent union. The manosphere addresses some of these issues but is expanding to address more. It's growing past its teenage rebellion — pick up artists, "game" and semi-misogynistic rantings — toward a movement of men who are demanding not just equality, but a better future for men in relationships, marriage and family.

# (2.) Robert Stark and Robert Lindsay talk Elliot Rogers. -June 10, 2014

**Robert Stark:** We were discussing this Eliot Rodger guy…for me, I live in Santa Barbara, so this was local. However, I believe that this was not just a local event – it was nationwide. When you first heard about this in the news, what was your initial reaction?

**Robert Lindsay:** A friend of mine came to me the next day – Sunday morning – on the Internet, and he said, "There's been another shooting." He wouldn't give me any details, but then I went and looked it up, and at first I didn't know much about it, so I didn't understand what was going on. I just figured it's another mass shooting, and I didn't really understand why. Then, over the next few days, the reasons came out because he sent in his manifesto.

RS: For a person to go out and shoot random people, or total strangers…well it would be one thing if someone went out and harmed someone who they knew they were angry at, but to go out and shoot random people, I think someone would have to be pretty mentally tormented.

RL: I really get tired of hearing the attitude that all these people are mentally ill, and we need to treat the mentally ill better. They say, "The problem isn't guns – the problem is crazy people." But the thing is – these people are often not mentally ill at all. You don't have to be mentally ill to grab a gun and try to shoot as many people as you can.

RS: I totally agree with you – I said mentally tormented, not mentally ill. Mental illness is something you are born with. Someone could start off relatively normal, but they could drive themselves insane. I think there is a distinction there.

RL: Well, that is exactly what this guy did! I read his manifesto, and up until age he was 11 or 12, he was rather shy, but other than that he was very normal, very happy, very sociable young boy. He was pretty healthy in his head as a young boy, and he just got more and more unhealthy as life went on.

RS: Yes, what he had was high-functioning Asperger's Syndrome. But high-functioning Asperger's Syndrome is not like schizophrenia. A lot of those people could function and be productive in society in the right environment. You read his manifesto. At what point in his life did he go from having a relatively normal childhood to where he ended up at?

RL: I think it all started at age 12. And it got really bad at age 13 and on into 14 – that's when it hit him really bad. He got far gone from age 11 to age 16. He turned into a completely different person.

RS: Would you say it was because of the bullying in middle school?

RL: Yes! That's what did it. And he couldn't be popular. He was popular up until age 11 or so…that was the first year of middle school. In that year, it was ok…and the girls were nice to him. In elementary school, there were certain requirements to be popular, and they were not hard for him to live up to, but then it started changing.

138

Now it wasn't like this when I was in 7th grade, but in 7th and 8th grade for Eliot, it was all about the guys who are liked by girls – the guys who are popular with the girls. And the girls were only hanging out with some of the guys, certain of the guys. The girls were all flocking to a few of the guys – the Alphas or whatever. When he first started junior high, he was pretty popular, but after a while, all the popular kids started shunning him and making fun of him, and all the girls started ridiculing him. People were tormenting him, every single day, all day long.

He would have to hide in a corner of the hallway until the hallways cleared, and that was the only way he could even get to class because people would run up to him and throw him into the lockers, or they would run up to him and steal his books out of his arms, and he would have to go chase them. They'd call him "faggot" and "weirdo."

RS: Do you think it is worse today in that regard than when you were in high school?

RL: Bullying wasn't that bad when I was in high school. But middle school was crazy! I wasn't one of the ones who got bullied all the time. I got bullied to some extent, but...I was one of the bullies too. It was bully or be bullied. I wasn't one of the real popular kids, but I wasn't one of the rejects either. I had a lot of friends! But I wasn't one of the cool kids, that's for sure.

But I wasn't so dorky that all the cool kids were beating up on me. The only ones who were beating up on me were these totally scummed out

139

sociopath types. This one guy who hated me…we actually had a fight, a fistfight in the 8th grade. But then I had a whole bunch of friends who were my guys, and they weren't losers, but they weren't the popular kids either. They were cool people. I hung out with them, and they were my buddies. I had this great big wide circle of friends. And then we tormented the geeked out guys. I would get together with one of my friends, and we would torment one of those nerdy guys.

RS: If you remember the Columbine shooting – was that the main reason that shooting happened?

RL: I believe the shooters were bullied. There was not a whole lot of bullying going on at my high school. There were a few guys who were totally geeked out – I mean insanely geeked out. They were the biggest geeks in the whole school. They were so geeked out that if you saw them walking across the quad even from 100 yards away, if you'd never seen them before, you would say, "Whoa! What a geek!" You know? These guys were like circus freaks.

RS: What's the deal with Asperger's anyway? People keep using the term to mean anyone who is introverted.

RL: Yes, that's really wrong. If you have any problems connecting to other people, if you have any social problems such as social phobia, if you have problems talking to people, problems relating to people…they automatically say you have Asperger's! And that is completely wrong, 100% wrong. And if people say you're weird, everyone says, "Oh, you must be an Aspie!" Well, no! There are lots and lots of really weird people ranging from a little bit weird to really, really weird, and they do not have Asperger's, not even 1%!

RS: So what are the actual symptoms of Asperger's?

RL: I don't know! I mean…they're weird, yes. But they are weird in certain particular ways, and they are introverted in particular ways. I think maybe I met one Aspie in my whole life, but I wasn't able to confirm that he was an Aspie. Well, he was weird; he was weird as Hell. I mean really, really weird! He…acted like a robot, and he seemed mean and angry and cold. If you tried to talk to him, he wouldn't even answer. So…he just seemed like a jerk – the biggest jerk you ever met! An antisocial person – he was just hostile! But apparently that was just his extreme introversion.

If you got him to talk at all, he would talk like a robot. And that's really weird because you don't often meet people who act like that. I mean you meet people who are shut down. You know how men sort of shut down their feelings? You know those guys who get into the macho thing, and they get this sort of monotone? Well, that's one thing, but this guy sounded like a machine! He sounded like a robot.

And one time one of the fluorescent lights in the library went on the blink, and it started blinking on and off. You know how those lights go? They start flashing on and off, going Buh Buh Buh Buh Buh? It's a little bit weird when those lights do that, sure, but this guy totally tripped on it!

141

He was staring at with a blank stare on his face like he was on acid. You don't normally see people tripping on a flashing light like they were on acid. He was...entranced by it. And that's an autistic symptom.

Now, whether he was happy or not, I don't know...but he functioned well enough...He was a computer genius, and they hired him to work on the computers in the library. Later he was going to college and had his own apartment. But he was a really schizoid type guy – he didn't relate to other people at all – a real loner. I think he was an Aspie! I haven't met any others, but that one I met was weird as Hell.

RS: With Eliot Rodger, people are saying he is a psychopath, but I don't think that's necessarily true.

RL: No! Absolutely not. I don't believe it because – let me tell you something. Up until age 11 or 12, and maybe – maybe – even afterwards, he was a relatively normal kid. There are some signs of pathology, but most kids are pathological. You notice over and over, reading his autobiography, how much emphasis he places on whether or not someone was kind and goodhearted and loving and nice. Over and over, he compliments people – for instance, he would say, "My teacher was very, very kind. She was a nice person." Psychopaths don't say that!

RS: I think with Eliot, if he were brought up in the right environment, he had the potential to be a basically decent and productive member of society.

142

RL: Well, there are guys who are about as Aspie as he was...and they do all right.

RS: You know, some people with mental illnesses...like schizophrenia... can be extremely violent...but in general, people who are on the autistic spectrum are usually pretty peaceful.

RL: Ummm, yes, but if you talk to people who know them or live with them...some of these guys have gotten married and have kids...they have these things called meltdowns on a fairly regular basis, and it's like a temper tantrum for adults. It's just...part of being an Aspie.

RS: I think the problem is that because they are unable to express themselves, that rage is bottled up like that.

RL: Their rage supposedly comes from frustration because they are pretty much frustrated all the time. They can't read other people, and other people can't relate to them, and there is this total miscommunication going on all the time. They are constantly having their needs thwarted. And people who have their needs thwarted all the time get pretty angry...as we can see in the case of Eliot Rodger!

RS: Regarding rage, Eliot had a number of incidents. In one of them, he went to a party near the university...

RL: Yes, initially he tried to talk to some people, but they weren't really talking to him. Before this, he would go to parties sometimes, and he would always get all isolated...standing up against the doorway or the

143

wall, and everybody else would be talking and socializing and smoking dope and drinking, and Eliot would be all isolated and alone and no one talking to him, and after a while, he would start to feel weird and leave.

But this time, he went up to some people and started talking to them, and I guess it didn't go very well, and then later he saw some Asian guy talking to a hot blond, and it really pissed him off. He decided to be really macho – he thought being macho would make him cool. He tried to be an Alpha. He walked right up to both of them, and he burned the guy, insulted him and pushed him aside, and then he got in next to the girl. And then both of them – the Asian guy and the blond girl – said, "Whoa! I think someone has had too much to drink!" And they got away from him.

Later on, he ended up on the lawn, and everyone else was having fun, and he was all alone on the lawn feeling like an idiot. The party went on, and Eliot ended up upstairs on the balcony, and I'm not sure if people were making fun of him or not – I don't really know – I think they were just ignoring him.

But he started getting angrier and angrier, and…I guess it was a 10 foot balcony? I don't know, if you fell from it, if you would get real hurt? I don't know what was on the ground below, if it was grass or maybe a lawn. Apparently you could push people off this ledge pretty easily. He tried to push some of the girls off the deck! And a bunch of the guys got really mad, and they started pushing him too, and there was a pushing and shoving match…and they…pushed him off the deck. And I think he broke his ankle?

RS: He said he got really hurt, and no one would help him.

RL: Well, what do you expect? Everyone at the party hated him! He started walking away, and the people next door were having a party themselves apparently in tandem with the people who were having the party where he was at. Apparently they knew what had happened, and they started yelling at him, calling him "faggot" and "idiot." I am not sure what happened, but a big fight ensued between Rodger and these guys, and…he got his ass beat by these guys. He got beat up. He got a broken leg. At some point as he was walking home, a girl helped him, but then he hobbled the rest of the way home. He was laid up with a broken leg for some time.

RS: Another thing that happened was he saw this couple on the beach, and he got some orange juice and sprayed super soakers on them.

RL: No, it was at a park, and it wasn't a couple, it was a whole group of young men and women who were having a blast on a Sunday afternoon. He was watching them, and he started getting more and more angry, so he went and got a soaker and some orange juice, and he came back, and he started spraying it all over them. The group got mad, and they chased Eliot. He ran all the way back to his car and jumped in his car and took off.

RS: The other thing about him was that he was mixed race himself, and he particularly disliked mixed couples.

RL: Actually…he doesn't talk much about that. I don't think he had a big complex about that.

RS: I think that in the PC media, being a racist is the worst thing, and his racism got a lot of attention in the media…

RL: Well, first of all, the media keeps saying that he had a complex about being Asian. Not really true. In his early years, he had a bit of a complex about being Asian because he wanted to fit in as all his friends were White, and those were the people he was trying to fit in with.

RS: Did he feel that he was looked down upon by Whites?

RL: I don't think so. They probably treated him better. White people treat minorities better if they are part-White. You see, nobody will ever admit to it, and I get called racist all the time for saying things like this, but let me tell you something! A Black person who is half-White will be treated a lot better by White people than a Black person who is all Black. A HAPA, a half-Asian, half-White, will be treated better by Whites than a full-blooded Asian.

The more White you have in you, the better White people treat you. That's just the way it goes! It's a simple fact! White nationalists probably would not agree with this, but the truth is that on some sort of a basic

146

level, White people will respect someone who has a lot of White in them. They love the person for that…

RS: I think because he was Whiter than some people…he saw an Indian guy and then a Mexican guy and then a Black guy and then a full Asian guy, all with blond White women, and he hated seeing that. His attitude was, "Why is it that these inferior races could get a blond White woman and I couldn't?"

RL: Well, you see, the thing is, everyone is saying that he had this big complex about being Asian, but…there are only a couple of references to that in the manifesto – when he was younger – but I think that at some point, maybe around age 12 or 13, he completely buried this aspect of himself. He just stuffed it – down into his subconscious. He repressed it. And from then on, he simply saw himself as fully White, as a White man, period.

RS: So was the issue that he felt that the White girls didn't view him as a White man?

RL: Noo…noo…he just…saw himself as a White man! His attitude was, "Hey, I'm White!" And he does look White. In his videos, he looks like a White guy. A lot of times, you cross a White and an Asian, and you end up with a…White! You cross a White with an Indian from India, often, you end up with a White person. White genes are pretty strong. They're not as recessive as everybody thinks. Either that, or there are some genes that are even more recessive than White genes.

147

RS: So you don't think the racial aspect of it is an issue.

RL: No! He doesn't even look Asian. And he identified as White. And he looks White.

RS: Ok, so why did he get so mad when he saw some interracial couples?

RL: Well. He saw himself as some sort of budding White nationalist! He saw himself as, "Hey, I'm White, and I am a superior man," and he thought Asians were inferior. He thought Asian guys were geeks and dweebs and idiots and fools. And he thought Black guys were complete animals – lowlifes.

RS: Yes, he made a big deal about how he was descended from British aristocracy...

RL: He was.

RS: He saw himself as better than other people.

RL: Yes, a really big part of him is that narcissism – that he needs to feel better than other people. That's his main pathology. And probably that more than anything else caused his rampage. If you want to blame anything, blame his narcissism.

RS: He fluctuated between having very high self-esteem and having very low self-esteem.

RL: What do you expect? Do you understand how narcissism works? I don't know if most people understand how narcissism works. In narcissism, we see these peaks and crashes. It's either they think they are the greatest person in the whole world, but if they are ever reminded that they are not the greatest person in the whole world, then they might crash and think they are the lowest worm that ever crawled the face of the Earth. It's either one or the other with these people. They can't be regular. He either has to be king of the world, or he has to be lowest slug you've ever seen.

Some people think that deep down inside, narcissists have very low self-esteem, and in order to compensate for that, they have to create this huge ego. See, basically, what people are trying to do is – they're trying to be normal. They are trying to get to that zero-state. They are trying to get to that...norm. They are trying to be ok. So when the narcissist is thinking, "I am the lowest worm that ever crawled the face of the Earth," he's -100 on an egotism scale. And you see...the farther down you are on that scale, the further up you have to go to be normal.

So if you're -100 on egotism, you have to go to +100 to feel normal. If you think you are the lowest slug on the face of the Earth, you have to think you are King of the Universe in order to even feel normal. You see? Someone who just feels a little bit inferior would only have to feel a little bit superior to feel normal. I think people are trying to achieve the norm. And the more down you feel, the more up you have to be to get to that norm. And that's why you see this bizarre fluctuating self-esteem in the narcissist where he's like I am the greatest man that ever lived or else I am absolutely worthless.

RS: There's a theory that he saw himself as the absolute gentleman, and when he saw girls with guys he viewed as lower than him, he thought those guys as obnoxious brutes.

RL: Well, yeah! That's the whole nice guy thing. The feminists and the anti-PUA/Game people on the Net are going crazy over this nice guy thing. They refer it as nice guys (TM). And they are all saying that in truth, nice guys aren't really very nice! Well…macho alphas who get all the women – they aren't very nice either, are they?

But the whole line is wrong. Nice guys are nice! That's what they are all about. And the attitude of the Manosphere is all about "nice guys finish last," and the biggest assholes – the Alphas – get all the women, and the nice guys get the leftovers. We have heard all these things many times before. Obviously, there is some truth to it. Now, I've been a nice guy my whole life, and I've done pretty well with women, but on the other hand, I'm not a real nice guy. I've been told that I look like a sexual threat, and that I give off the appearance of someone who was experienced…with women.

RS: Don't forget those serial killer glasses. You got rid of those. You got new glasses.

RL: Well…it's not so much that women don't like a nice guy, but more that they like a guy who has a sense of danger.

150

RS: Well…but Eliot turned out to be pretty dangerous…

RL: He didn't look dangerous. He looked harmless. He keeps calling himself a mouse over and over in that manifesto of his. He says, "They treated me like I was a mouse…I felt like an insignificant little mouse." So this is really a classic case of some guy who feels completely inferior – who feels like a mouse – and in order to compensate for that, he has to feel like a king…like God! He felt so low that even being King of the World wasn't enough for him…he had to become God! He became God. I am God, destroyer of worlds!

RS: His fantasy was becoming a dictator and putting all women in concentration camps…and starving them to death while he watched them die…

RL: And in the end, he did become a God, did he not? Right? Wasn't he that night, when he was shooting people…wasn't he God? Who can take your life away, Robert?

RS: Yes, I see what you mean. I see what you are getting at.

RL: Only God can give life, and only God can take life. And you know, I have talked to people who told me that they liked to fantasize about killing people…they told me that they were never going to do it, but it was sort of fun to think about it…and when they thought like this, they felt huge, 1000 feet tall, like God.

RS: You don't have to answer this, but have you ever fantasized about killing people?

RL: Yes, of course, sure. Yes, I have. You know, I have fantasized about killing my enemies, and even, I even have fantasized about doing what Eliot did! I think a lot of us have, really.

RS: A lot of people fantasize about killing their enemies, but some people also fantasize about obliterating large numbers of human beings, of strangers.

RL: Sure, sure, of course. You know, you are driving down the street, and you look over, and there's a sidewalk filled people, and you fantasize you have an AK-47 and some hand grenades…and you start firing the gun, and then you start throwing the hand grenades! You know, I have told people that I have thought about stuff like that, and at least with guys, they usually start laughing and say, "Yeah, so have I." And these are guys who work in offices, wear ties, sit at a desk…

RS: But now, if you talk about that, you will be put on some watchlist.

RL: Well, look! Everybody thinks about things like that every now and then…but they aren't serious. But if you are actually thinking about it like it is something you really, really want to do…that's…completely different. I mean I thought about that stuff, but I knew that I wasn't going to do it. You know?

RS: Have you ever felt like Eliot Rodger at some point in your life?

152

RL: Ummm. Yes. Yes. I have, yes.

RS: At his age, or...?

RL: It was more when I was older than he was. You know what? I can understand the guy's feelings! If people don't treat you nice, if everybody is sort of treating you like crap, you just...you sort of...you want to kill them! You want to kill the people who don't treat you right. What people want is, as Carl Rogers said, unconditional positive regard.

They don't want people communicating that there is something wrong with them, that they are weird, that you are screwed up...that's all...it's basically rejection. You know really – people should be careful about rejecting other people! Because when you reject someone, the basic primitive instinct of the person who you rejected is..."I'm going to kill you!" You know? Just for doing that to me, just for rejecting me. You insulted me!

RS: And there is a distinction between sexual rejection and social rejection. I think someone who is being sexually rejected but has a healthy enough social life is probably going to be ok. I think the problem is a combination of sexual and social rejection.

RL: Hey! Social life is very important! If you are at the point in your life where nobody's even being friendly to you...nobody's talking to you... you're not talking to anyone...you don't have any friends...you don't talk to any people on the phone...nobody comes over...you don't go visit anybody...I mean, that's a pretty bad place to be! It's lonely. It's really,

really lonely! You feel like you are all alone in the whole world. You've never felt so lonely in your life!

I've felt that way a few times when I moved to a new city...You see all these new people everywhere you go – total strangers – and you don't know what to say to them! What are you going to say? Really, what you ought to be able to do is say, "Hi, I just moved to this town, and I don't know a soul in this whole place. You want to be friends?" But you can't do that! See? But you know? You really ought to be able to do something like that. I mean, what are you going to do?

You move to a whole new city all alone, and you don't know one single person! But if you walk up to someone and say, "Hey, I just moved to this town all alone, and I do not know one single person in this whole town. You want to be friends?" Well, you're considered to be weird! You're weird! The problem is you are making yourself vulnerable, and that's not really accepted.

People act like you move to a whole new town all alone, and within 24 hours, you are supposed to have a whole bunch of new friends. But if you say, "Hey, I just moved here. I don't know a soul" ...you're pitiful! You know what? We're not very nice! There are a lot of lonely people in our country, and we're not very nice to them! People say, "Huh? What's wrong with you? How come you can't make friends? Why don't you just go make some friends?"

That ain't right. A lot of people have a hard time making friends, and they're really lonely, and it shouldn't be a shameful thing to say that you're lonely or you don't have any friends or, "Hey, you want to make friends?" It shouldn't be a source of shame. And we have made it into a source of shame!

RS: These mass shootings – it seems to be largely an American phenomenon. There have been a few in other countries, but by and large, it seems to be largely an American thing.

RL: Well. We're the ones who let everyone have a gun, right?

RS: Well, other countries let you have a gun. I think it is something about American society that is different…

RL: Well. How many other countries let you have a semi-automatic weapon?

RS: In Switzerland, everyone has a gun.

RL: Do they let you have automatic weapons?

RS: I don't know about that.

RL: Well, ok. You know, these automatic weapons come in awful handy for these mass shootings.

RS: In China, there have been some people going berserk with knives. The was a story about a 40-year-old man going into an elementary school in China and chopping up a bunch of kids.

RL: Yes. There was another guy who went berserk with a bulldozer on a street, on a sidewalk. Well, you know, people will use whatever is handy for a weapon. But those semi-automatic weapons, they sure do make it easier!

RS: So what are your thoughts about the PUAHate site that Eliot was hanging out on?

RL: Oh! Yes. I went there! I went there before it got famous due to this Eliot Rodger thing. I went there a number of months ago. Well, on that site…these guys are really angry! And their whole thing is like, "We're not getting any women! We're all like, incels." I don't know if all of them have been virgins their whole lives or if they are just temporarily incel, which is no source of shame!

I mean I am temporarily incel right now. I've been temporarily incel many times in my life. I am at the moment. Maybe I have been temporarily incel now for…three months? It's not the end of the world, you know? I mean everybody goes through this…but, at what point does incel become not normal and become Incel with a capital I? Anyway, about the PUAHate site, there are these guys on there, and they're not getting any women, and a lot of them have spent a lot of money on these PUA con artists. They went to these boot camp things, or they bought all these tapes and videos.

RS: Some of those guys have spent thousands and thousands of dollars. I remember a while back, there was a similar shooting. There was a guy named George Sodini who shot up a gym for basically the same reason that Eliot Rodger did. He spent thousands of dollars on these pickup artist seminars.

RL: Yes, they can cost up to $3,000 to $5,000...to $10,000.

RS: And a lot of those guys are basically con artists.

RL: Of course they are con artists! Most of these PUA guys charging you for stuff are...classic con artists. They're sociopaths. Narcissists, sociopaths, whatever...I mean that sort of thing was guaranteed...as soon as that PUA stuff came out, you knew a bunch of con artists were going to flock to that industry. That industry has a great big welcome mat, a giant flashing neon sign that says, "Con artists, come here! Con artists, right this way!" You know? It was perfectly designed for those types. And a lot of the biggest PUA guys...are con artists themselves... especially the ones who are charging you. They're great big huge liars. They're not ok people.

RS: What do you think of the media accusations where they say that the misogyny of the Manosphere is responsible for contributing to Eliot's spree?

RL: Well, first of all...the United States is not a particularly misogynistic country on a worldwide basis, is it?

RS: Not at all. It is probably the least misogynistic country if you compare it to the rest of the world.

RL: Probably one of the least. Misogyny is much worse in Latin America, Sub-Saharan Africa, the Arab World, Iran, Pakistan, India, Nepal, and Bangladesh. What about Southeast Asia? I don't know. In Japan, in China. Misogyny is the way of the world. In most of the world, women are second-class citizens. That's just...normal.

RS: Would you say that those Manosphere sites like Roissy are misogynistic?

RL: Yes! Yes, Roissy's site. Roissy is a misogynist, and his commenters are worse than he is, and they're just feeding off each other. That whole scene is just...insanely misogynistic, really. But it's not like Roissy doesn't say things that are true...

RS: So what does Roissy say that is true?

RL: Well...a lot of what those guys are saying is true, and a lot of what misogynists say is true, unfortunately. A lot of what women who hate men say about men is true. But...both of them...they're only seeing half the picture. I mean, there's a huge downside to women. 50% of women is like a downside, and the other 50% is like an upside.

RS: You've been a misogynist at some point in your life.

RL: Yes, I got into that for a while. But it was odd, coming from a guy who had always loved females from an early age. I always just loved females. I never thought about it, never thought about the philosophy of it, whether it made sense philosophically or scientifically or whether females deserve to be hated or deserve to be loved...I just simply decided that I loved them, and that was that.

RS: When did you get into the misogyny thing?

RL: Well, it happened when I got older. I had worked myself into a bad state to where a lot of women were rejecting me, rejecting me for being weird. They were always like, "Whoa! You're weird, dude." Like that. And...I started hating them for that. Sort of like Eliot Rodger!

RS: This is a little bit off-topic, but you mentioned that you were racist for a while.

RL: Yes, I got into that for a while. I got into anti-Semitism. I don't even know how it happened because I was always a Jew-lover, a Judeophile, my whole life. I loved Jews like i loved females, I never thought about it, I never analyzed it. Did Jews deserve to be loved? Did they deserve to be hated?

I came from a family of strong Judeophiles, and I was always like, "Woohoo! I love Jews!" You know? But then, in 2001, when the Israelis were shooting up Bethlehem, and they were shooting up the church where Jesus was born...You know, I'm a Christian! And those PLO guys were staying in the church, hiding there. And those Jews, even in the church where Jesus was born, they were killing people! They were murdering them!

RS: I think with the anti-Semitism thing and the misogyny thing, I know a lot of guys, when they first discover these things…or people in general, when they first discover stuff, they go through a phase where they are really angry or maybe racist or misogynistic, but after a while, they calm down, and they come to accept the group for what they are. Do you think that is true?

RL: I suppose, but I went the opposite way. I was raised to be non-racist! We were all raised to be non-racist. One time at the dinner table, I remember, one of us brothers said the word "nigger."

RS: Was it you?

RL: I don't know! I don't remember who said it. It wasn't the sort of word I used much back then. But, oh man! My father! My father just freaked out! I mean, all these Blacks and anti-racists who say "All Whites are racist," how do they explain my father? He shut down the whole dinner right there. He made it clear that we were never, ever to use that word at the dinner table again. Why did my father shut down that whole dinner table conversation because someone said nigger? My Dad – he's a racist?

RS: You said you called a guy that term once. You called him a nigger.

RL: Yes, I did. I did it. I was mad at him. We were having a fight. This Black guy and I were having this big huge fight, and I called him a nigger. I don't know. I don't feel bad about it. I'll call anyone anything that they deserve to be called if I am mad enough…

160

RS: Sure, when you are in a fight with someone, you want to find the worst thing that you can possibly call that person.

RL: Of course. You're going to look for their ethnicity, their race, their gender – if it's a woman, you're going to call her a cunt. If they're gay, you're going to call him a faggot. If they're a different race, you're going to call them nigger or beaner or spic or whatever. Or even a different ethnicity! If he's an Arab, you call him a towelhead, if he's French, you call him a frog. You just have to dig into your bag of tricks and find some appropriate insult and throw it at them.

If you're mad enough…if you and this other person are ready to punch each other, it's perfectly acceptable to whip out the insults. If you do that, I don't think it indicates how you feel deep down inside at all! That's the anti-racist line, and it's completely wrong!

RS: Exactly!

RL: It doesn't mean you're bigoted, or racist or sexist or homophobic. It just means you're mad!

RS: So going back to the previous topic, these spree shootings seem to be becoming more and more common. Why do you think they are becoming more common?

RL: You mean the mass killings?

RS: Mass killings, yes. Like this Eliot Rodger case.

161

RL: Well...probably...they're getting a lot of play in the media! And psycho-type people are looking at that and deciding to do it. It's a case of "the more there are, the more there are," you know what I mean? It's like a suicide epidemic. A few people do it, then more people start doing it, and then, the more there are, the more there are! The more people are doing it, the more people think this is a cool thing to do. The behavior feeds off itself. It's a vicious circle. It creates more of itself just by being there. The more of it there is, the more of it it spurs on, you know?

RS: Do you think this incel thing is more common than it was in the past?

RL: I don't know! I grew up with a lot of guys who weren't getting laid, so...it was pretty common. It was just normal. A lot of guys weren't getting laid. It was almost...to be expected. It was like, "Of course you're not having any sex. Well, you're not married, right?" It might be weird that he's not married, but the fact that he's not married, and he's not having any sex was not getting any sex was not considered weird at all. It was acknowledged that a few guys who weren't married could get some sex but unmarried guys...back then – it was expected that you weren't having sex. It was even harder then.

RS: I remember you wrote an article after the George Sodini case predicting that more guys would go nuts like that guy did.

RL: Yes. And it happened, right? And…there's going to be more, even after this Eliot Rodger guy. We have not seen the end of this!

RS: So do you consider sex to be a necessary component of living a happy and effective life?

RL: Well, yes. But in a certain way, it isn't like your needs for survival. It's not like shitting and pissing and eating and drinking. If you quit sleeping, you're going to die! If you quit shitting and pissing, you're going to die. Without water, you can live for maybe three days. If you quit eating food, at some point, you're just going to die. If you quit having sex, you're not going to die!

RS: You wrote that these modern feminists are saying that these incel guys may just have to go years, decades or possibly their whole lives without sex.

RL: Yes, well, that's exactly what they are saying, isn't it? Isn't that precisely what they are saying on these feminist sites? What are they saying? The feminists are saying, "Look! You guys have no right to sex! You're entitled. You think you have a right to have sex." The thing is, to these feminists, it is perfectly acceptable for a guy to go years, decades or even a lifetime without having sex with a woman because he had no right to sex! And he had no right to feel entitled that way.

And women have the right to turn down men…all the time! For a year, or a decade, or a lifetime. That's their right. That's women's right. And

163

some of you guys – you're just going to lose out, and that's just the way it goes. Because we're the sexual gatekeepers.

And...you know...? That's not an attitude...that's going to fly very well! Tell you what. You go say that to a bunch of incel guys. Tell them, "Hey look. Women say you have no right to sex, and you're going to get it whenever they decide to give it to you, and...you just might never get it! Because...maybe they just don't feel like giving it to you!"

You know? You think that's going to go over with those guys? You think these incel guys are just going to say, "Oh. Ok. Well, whether we get sex or not depends on whether the women want to give it to us. Ok. And maybe I'll go my whole life and never have sex because...chicks just don't feel like giving it to me, and that's just a-ok!" You think these incels are going to react that way?

RS: What should the attitude of society be towards this issue?

RL: Well, it wasn't always this way.

RS: To wrap up the show, do you have any final words about Eliot Rodger.

RL: Yes, I would like to make a complaint. Notice how the feminists and their male buddies are all running around screaming, "Misogyny! Misogyny! We have to stop this horrible misogyny!" Yes, there is misogyny in our culture. Well...why was Eliot Rodger a misogynist?

164

Because…as a boy, he was not a misogynist. He turned into one! Why did he turn into a misogynist?

RS: And what would you say the reason he turned into a misogynist was?

RL: Well. Women turned him into a misogynist! They hated him, they insulted him, they humiliated him, they ignored him, and…that's what did it. I mean you can say that he shouldn't have reacted that way, but… people who experience mass rejection, they tend to get…pretty mad.

RS: Before wrapping up, I would like to discuss one more thing. One of the interesting things about Eliot Rodger is…I mentioned a guy like Roissy…See, the difference between those two is that Eliot Rodger hated promiscuous men as much as he hated promiscuous women. But these guys like Roissy – they actually celebrate promiscuous men, but they hate promiscuous women. Well, they don't hate the women – they just have a low opinion of them. That is a key difference between those two. Eliot Rodger was…he was really a misanthrope, not just a misogynist.

RL: Well, yes, he got to the point where he hated men just as much as he hated women. And the first three people he killed were…fellow incels, probably. Those three Chinese guys who he said were total nerds, well – they weren't getting any pussy either from what I understand.

RS: Yes, they probably had more in common with him than he would have admitted.

RL: Right, right. He hated those guys because they were nerds! That guy just hated everybody, man. And he was going to kill his own Mom and his own brother. His Mom was very good to him, and his brother was very good to him too. The only person he didn't want to kill was his father. He hated the whole world. He hated you. He hated me. He was going to try to kill you. He was going to try to kill me. The Hell with him!

# (3.) Robert Stark interviews Santa Barbara Mayoral Candidate Hal Conklin. -Aug 7, 2017

**[Robert Stark]** What are the key issues that inspired you to run for mayor in the upcoming election and what do you see as the biggest problems facing the city?

**[Hal Conklin]** With the turnover of almost all of the City Council, there is little institutional memory left, nor any leadership devoted to bringing the community together in a dialogue on the future of our city. Santa Barbara has had a long history of citizen involvement in its future stretching from its historic preservation of architecture after the 1925 earthquake, to the restoration of its waterfront and downtown in the 1980's, to the creation of its cultural institutions in the first decade of the 21st century. Where is that leadership for the future??

We need to return to giving the whole community a voice. It is the peoples' voice – not the voice of the City Council – which needs to speak with clarity and inspiration. The Mayor may be in the role as the orchestra leader, but it is the orchestra itself (the people) which makes the music! The Mayor needs to be the "mediator" of dialogue – giving everyone the opportunity to voice their concerns, hopes and desires. Too often it just becomes the voice of special political interests.

Our country is living through a period of division that could tear us apart. While our national leadership fights among itself saying "NO" to everything, we need to build Santa Barbara as a model community that says' "YES" to supporting one another moving forward. We need to roll up our sleeves and bring our citizens together in unity, and I am committed to being the kind of Mayor that will work tirelessly to see that this is done.

**As the former mayor of Santa Barbara what were your biggest accomplishments as mayor?**

Among others:

- Saved Stearns Wharf from being torn down and raised the funds to have it restored and put back in service
- Created the Santa Barbara Cultural District (sometimes referred to as the Historic Theater District) that stretched from De La Guerra Street to Sola Street, and from Chapala Street to Santa Barbara Street. We funded the restoration of the Museum of Art, launched the creation of the Santa Barbara Center for the Performing Arts (Granada Theater), improvements to the Arlington Theater, and brought restaurants and street art to the district.
- I was a member of the three-person committee that oversaw the development of Paseo Nuevo to bring retail sales back to downtown Santa Barbara.
- Created a process of public involvement that tackled and reduced gang violence in the city
- Made the Arts and protecting the Environment my top priorities

**As the President of USA Green Communities, what have been some of your accomplishments with that organization and what are your plans to make Santa Barbara more eco-friendly and energy independent?**

With the help of the Institute for Local Government (ILG) in Sacramento, of which I am still a Board member, and with the help of the Bren School at UCSB, we developed a set of ten criteria for sustainability against which cities could be measured to determine their commitment to sustainable practices. These included criteria for water, energy, transportation, product purchasing, recycling, etc. When a city achieves one complete program in each of these areas they would are rewarded with a Silver designation. If they achieve three programs in each of these ten areas, they get a Gold certification. When they have reached six programs in each of these ten areas, they receive a Platinum certification. Currently, we have 115 cities in the program in California that are being reviewed and certified by the ILG, and through USA Green Communities we are putting graduate level interns in many of these cities to add practical experience to their studies.

**You have a strong passion for historic preservation. Is most of the Spanish Colonial architecture that was built in the early 20th Century protected by Historic Preservation laws? Is Mid Century modern architecture the most vulnerable to demolition and in need of protection?**

169

Santa Barbara led the nation following the 1925 earthquake in developing and implementing historic standards for the preservation of history and architecture. It wasn't until the 1980's that the Historic Landmarks Committee process was enacted into law and put in the Charter of the City. Many people come to Santa Barbara because they like what they see, but when they go to develop property, they do not like the process. It is an interesting "give and take" dynamic community conversation that has a lot of subjectivity built into it. Nevertheless, it has created a wonderful mix of preservation and replicated history. Mid Century architecture is part of the guidelines for historic preservation.

**What are your thoughts on the Average Unit-Size Density program which allows developers to increase density in exchange for providing a certain number of affordable units? Do you see increasing density a solution to housing costs?**

AUD is a good tool for building more so-called "affordable" housing. It needs to be focused though, on where it is most appropriate and where it is needed the most – namely downtown. Having a greater mix of residents downtown is part of the next generation of what a downtown needs to create in order to sustain itself. Unfortunately, up to now, the City Council has taken a "hands off" policy until a certain number of units are built. I think the City has to have a much more proactive response so that the public sees the immediate benefit of housing for workers. If all that gets built first are upscale condos, then the public could easily rise up and throw the whole program out the window.

Everyone thought that lower Chapala Street would be a good place for worker housing, but what we ended up with was mostly more expensive condos ranging up to $3,000,000 each.

**Many students struggle to pay rent and that puts further strain on the rental market. Would you support incentivizing Santa Barbara City College and UCSB to build more student housing on campus?**

I would certainly provide incentives for City College to build more housing, but it needs to be a community process to determine when, where, and how big each project is to become. Without citizen involvement from the start, the project will be killed by negative public opinion. As for UCSB, I think housing needs to be within walking distance. If we provide incentives for UCSB housing that add to the auto traffic, it would be a nightmare.

**Even though the city of Santa Barbara itself has a greenbelt what are your thoughts on the argument that infill development prevents further sprawl into neighboring regions?**

Infill development always occurs, but the traffic impacts have to be known by the community well in advance. The citizens have voted twice for a level of circulation, and the "experts" at City Hall often see it differently for good and practical reasons. In the end though, the citizens of the city have the final say, and if City Hall loses trust with the voters, they will just shut down any infill development. A community-wide planning process is critical to the success of more density.

**Most new rental units tend to be expensive one or two bedroom units. Do you support incentivizing a variety of new housing units ranging from micro apartments for students and several bedroom units for families?**

Right now the City owns or controls over 10% of the housing stock in Santa Barbara. With the help of the Housing Authority as the control agent, it's possible to manage the rental rates so that most, if not all, units stay affordable. We should use the Housing Authority to build micro apartments on the parking lots below the bluffs at City College and more rental units downtown for workers and families. You can only get away with more density if you reduce the need to drive, so the housing has to be adjacent to where people need to go to school or work.

**Santa Barbara has very strict height limits and there has been pressure to restrict heights even further. However it is important to point out that many of Santa Barbara's great landmarks including the Court House Clock Tower, The Arlington Theater, and The Grenada Theater could not get built with today's height limits. Would you support allowing for taller structures if they conform to an aesthetic standard and what should be the official height limit? The hotel next to the Historic El Paseo is a great example of a structure that is fairly tall yet conforms to a historic aesthetic standard. I see the key issue as good design rather than height.**

The 60 ft. height standard was voted into the City Charter in the 1960's and it cannot be changed by anyone except at the ballot box. Based on previous attempts to do so, the chances of that succeeding are slim to none. Whether or not I think it is a good idea, there are some issues that are worth fighting over, and others that are not. I would look for more practical ways to approve projects.

**There are several massive parking lots downtown. On one hand they create convenient parking for visitors and shoppers but also take up a lot of valuable land creating pedestrian dead zones along Anacapa and De La Vina. Would you support turning those parking lots into mix used projects with Paseos and relocating the parking underground?**

Based upon what it cost to build underground parking at the Granada lot, the cost per space is prohibitive. In order to do it, you either have to put in a massive subsidy from the taxpayers (e.g.- the old Redevelopment Agency or the current Parking Authority), or you have to allow very expensive condos to subsidize it. I think our first priority should be modest housing for workers downtown, and expensive condos just add to the problem.

**What are your thoughts on the situation between the police and the homeless on State Street? On one hand there are the concerns about civil liberties and the criminalization of homelessness while others are more concerned about the homeless harming business**

**and tourism. How do you address these issues and do you see the key as finding the right balanced approach?**

Unfortunately, I have been through too many court cases over this issue, and I realize how frustrating it is to deal with people panhandling. I am a big believer in providing alternative housing and services to people on the street, but I also have little tolerance for bad behavior. Having a son who has run a home for alcoholic and drug offenders, I am convinced more than ever that we need a concerted effort of education and partnership between the merchants, tourist outreach, the City and the Police to discourage the giving of money to panhandlers on the street. Once the money dries up, the "problem" people on the street will move on to more lucrative environments.

**The city council recently voted for a measure for the public to vote on a sales tax increase. Do you support the measure? What are your thoughts on the argument that sales taxes disproportionately affect the working class and harm the tourism industry?**

I do support allowing the voters to decide whether or not this is a worthy idea and a good source of money. I think this has to be accompanied by a well-designed set of benchmarks and scoreboards that let the public know on a regular basis whether or not we are achieving our goals and objectives. There is no easy answer that is totally fair in terms of how you achieve these goals of a new Police Station or repairing our roads, but to put it off forever because the perfect solution hasn't come along will lead to more and more frustration and anger.

**Do you have an official budget proposal and what do you see as the biggest areas of waste in the city's budget?**

I have to admit that I have studied the City's budgeting process more than 99% of the people in Santa Barbara, and I tend to look at anyone who tells me they have a new budget proposal with a fair degree of skepticism. The priorities of the Budget (outside of special funds such as the Harbor, Airport, etc.) are always public safety first, followed by basic infrastructure, and then finally, social services including parks and recreation. The biggest issue with the Budget is that it is almost impossible for the average citizen to see how the money is being spent. It isn't that we need a line-item budget so that everyone can take pot-shots at it, but rather the budget needs to be tied to measureable indicators so that the public knows whether or not they are getting what they believe they are paying for. In a Budget where the public is in the dark about what is happening, they tend to become frustrated and "assume" that money is being wasted. We need to have good salaries that attract good police and fire personnel, but we also need a transparent process of budgeting.

**What are your thoughts on proposals to generate revenue for the City? There are alternative proposals and solutions to generate revenue including a recent op ed in the Santa Barbara News Press by Frank Sanitate advocating for a County run Public Bank and**

175

**proposals to tax offshore oil revenue which has been done in Alaska. Do you see any of those proposals as viable?**

There are a lot of great hypothetical proposals that people put on the table, but in many cases this requires voter approval at the ballot box. The voters have voted numerous times to restrict oil development in the city's jurisdiction, so doing anything that suggests we use oil revenue is a fantasy. A County Public Bank is an interesting idea, but once again it might have to go before the voters and the city cannot spend any taxpayer dollars to promote it. If we are going to look at any ideas for revenue generation, the first place to look would be to the other 480 cities in California and see what they have been able to make work. We should look at all ideas, but the public wants to see results, not pie-in-the-sky ideas that then get shot down. We would be better off taking a good idea from another city where the idea works rather than speculating on an idea that has a limited chance of success.

**Do you support increasing the number of hotel unites as a way to generate tax revenue rather than raising taxes on locals?**

I am in favor of more visitor serving uses, as long as it fits within the existing zoning and coastal plan. I am not in favor of extending a lot of visitor serving uses into peoples' neighborhoods without their permission. Ultimately, each neighborhood "owns" their own destiny, and we don't need "smart planning" City Council members thinking they are smarter that the citizens who elected them.

**What do you see as solutions to the vacant storefronts on Lower State Street? Should the land owners be required pay a vacancy fee? What are your thoughts on opening up the unused storefronts to local artist?**

There are many cities that have tackled this problem creatively. One way I favor would be to put an ordinance in place that requires that if a building is left vacant for more than sixty days, then the owner needs to work with a local arts or historical entity to allow a creative display for their window. If they leave the property vacant without a display for longer than 90 days, and the property becomes a public attraction for the homeless to sleep in their doorways, then the owner should be required to donate a monthly fee to the local homeless shelters.

**What are some of your economic proposals to bring new jobs to Santa Barbara? What can be done to attract more well-paying middle class jobs to the city? Should we focus on luring existing industries or create new industries?**

One of the greatest sources of new ideas that lead to new jobs are the universities and colleges in our area. We should have their various departments tied into an economic development plan for the city. With a variety of good ideas coming in the forms of environmental protection from the Bren School, or economic development opportunities from the nano-technology divisions, or a host of others, we should be creatively finding incentives to plant these new ideas in business locations within the city limits or on the airport property. The City's economic development programs have most often been passive. It is time for a proactive partnership formally implemented.

**The transit system in Santa Barbara is currently reliant on bus transit which is often slow and not accessible for many commuters. For example there is not a direct way to get from upper State Street to City College or from Upper State Street directly to the waterfront. What are your plans for bus transit?**

While the City does not have any authority over the Metropolitan Transit Authority, it does have the power to appoint members to their Board. It also has the power of persuasion to bringing the MTA to the table for long-ranging community planning. Tactical implementation of transit should be tied at the hip to community planning and the City Council and the neighborhoods should annually review and approve a plan that advances the City's long-term objectives.

**You have expressed interest in a light rail system. It would make the most sense to have either a light rail or monorail connecting downtown to UCSB with multiple stops in between including City College. Does Santa Barbara have the density for mass transit to be viable and do you see creating transit oriented developments along the stops as a solution to that?**

I don't know what is technologically possible today – or in the future – but I do believe we need to "think outside the box." State Street downtown, outer State Street, and Hollister Ave. are all one long direct

178

corridor, and it could easily accommodate a light rail corridor, especially if we reach a point with new energy technologies that would eliminate the need for overhead power lines. Five years ago, there was no such thing as a mass-produced hydrogen car. Five years from now, we might have the ability to power light rail trains with hydrogen propulsion. A "horizontal elevator" of non-polluting, efficient, and frequent transit would transform the ability to move people anywhere along the route, through the high-tech Goleta corridor, and out to UCSB.

***This is the only proper review of Stark's film:***

# James J O'Meara Reviews The Poet & The Cat. -May 15, 2015

*The Poet & The Cat*

Directed by Robert Stark

Written by Paul Bingham

Starring: Robert Stark & Charles E. Lincoln II

 If you're a fan of losers and serial killers, and enjoy the Alt-Right despaircore writings of Andy Nowicki or Paul Bingham, you've probably said, "Gee, I wish I could visit them at home, see them writing away on a rickety plywood table under the light in the kitchen, interacting with their cat and drinking a glass of Two Buck Chuck!"

Well, thanks to Robert Stark, and YouTube, now you can!

*The Poet & The Cat* stars Robert as the poet undergoing a quarter-life crisis (which is a new one on me, but apparently is a thing), and Charles E. Lincoln II is the cat; that is, the voice of the cat, who sounds distractingly like Judaic radio show crank Mark Levin, especially when he starts ranting in German. The cat, I mean.

It's fun to see Robert bring the poetry-scribbling loser to life, and the cat is a hoot as he ventriloquizes Bingham's bleak worldview.

"You're like a woman, you know.  You come at me shadowboxing, both paws extended; only then do the claws come out, and dig in so deeply."

The "feline Mephistopheles" insistently tries to draw the poet's thoughts from working his ordinary life problems into art and toward mass murder as the real path to fame, money and women; while constantly becoming distracted by the urge to hunt a mouse or complain about having been fixed.

"Just move like a cat. You're good at that.  All you girlfriends say you can be a creep."

Suffering *weltschmerz* after reading too many Hopeless Books? Feeling like a Delta Male after checking out too many man-o-sphere blogs?  Ignore that clickbait at Salon or HuffPo, and go here for a quarter-hour of someone else's entertaining quarterlife crisis.

## AFTERWORD BY BRANDON ADAMSON

"Can you take a picture of me eating this?" Robert
asked.

I don't remember what precise Asiatic seafood dish he
had ordered that day at PF Chang's, as our trip to Las
Vegas was finally winding down, but the battery in
Stark's precious camera had long since died, and so
I'd grown accustomed to entertaining his relentless
photographic demands. He was, I discovered, a
picture taking maniac.

"Can you get a picture of the Riviera sign?" "Now take
a picture of me standing in front of the sign." "Okay,
can you take another picture of me in front of the sign
from this angle." On and on for hours the process was
repeated, along nearly every block of the strip. Stark
would take note of every architectural or tidbit and
insist on at least one picture of it. The way I describe
experience, I know it almost sounds as if I'm talking
about a photo shoot with an aging diva, not unlike
Gina Gershon's character in Showgirls...but no this is
about Robert Stark, an underground artist, journalistic
legend in the flesh and most of all a man whose
passions are driven by aesthetics.

One of the first places we met up and explored on
that trip to Vegas in 2016 was the Miracle Mile shops
and emporiums. Neither of us had any idea at the
time, but those places would turn out to be the
inspiration for the setting of what I consider to be the
definitive scene of Stark's novel "Journey to Vapor
Island." The scene I'm referring to takes place at "The

Erotic Emporium," but you'll have to read the book if you'd like to find out what actually goes on there.

Over the course of our three day trip, we did a great deal of walking around. I was recovering from some kind of mild, undiagnosed respiratory/sinus infection, which left my energy reserves depleted right out of the gate. The heat was intense and at times barely tolerable, and this is coming from someone who has lived in Phoenix, Arizona for over 20 years. Had I not had a partner in crime depending on me, I probably would have been content to just jack off in my air conditioned 23rd floor room at The Flamingo, while occasionally moseying down to the casino to play some Money Mad Martians slot machines and eyeball the many random chicks coming and going through the lobby, all the while daydreaming about scandalous affairs that I was too lazy to even attempt to make happen.

As Stark and I walked along the strip and through the maze of casino corridors, we covered a lot of conversational ground as well. Robert frequently relayed anecdotes about various alternative political figures he had met and interviewed over the years. He had stories about the late Jonathan Bowden, whom he met shortly before Bowden's untimely death. Stark recounted memories of meeting all kinds of other guests as well, from proto-Alt-Right personalities (some newcomers, some long goners) to Johnny-one-note internet cranks, while always taking care not to share any personal or sensitive info. Stark even told me a humorous story about a prominent white nationalist refusing to eat Chinese food at an event he once attended. He relayed this to me as we were eating Indian food at the Las Vegas Fashion Show Mall food court. Naturally, Robert requested I take a photo of him devouring his meal (he is an annoyingly loud eater by the way, just saying.)

Over the course of knowing Robert Stark, I've come to respect him a great deal. For a low key, unassuming guy, he has managed to score and conduct in-depth and engaging interviews with nearly anybody who's anybody in underground politics and fringe culture over the course of the last 10 years. The Stark Truth podcast is the politcal equivalent of one of those 1970's-80s TV talent shows that celebrities would often appear on before they became famous. I'm talking hundreds, perhaps even thousands of prominent up and coming individuals. Here's just a small eclectic sampling of people whom Robert has interviewed:

Aleksandr Dugin, Al Lowe, Tila Tequila, Richard Spencer, Zoltan Istvan, Jim Goad, Richard Wolstencroft, Adam Parfrey, Ilana Mercer, Augustus Invictus, Adam Mayer, Keith Preston, En Ensh, Ronnie Martin, James Howard Kunstler, Adam Hengels, Anthony Hamilton…

For context, I myself have been a guest on Stark's program several times to promote various projects and have co-hosted the show on at least 40 or 50 occasions. The cumulation of these episodes only make up a tiny fraction of the overall number of completed podcasts filed away in Stark's vault. That should give you an idea of the sheer magnitude of Robert's journalistic body of work.

For outsiders, it can be difficult to pin down Stark's political ideology. One of the reasons for this is his non-confrontational interviewing style. He has a tendency to appear as though he's agreeing with whomever he's interviewing. Many radio shows and podcasts have a debate format, where the host spars with guests and generally takes a hostile, combative tone. In Stark's case, he makes his guests and their ideas the focus of the show, rather than making it about himself or trying to score points. In that sense it is similar to programs like Coast to Coast. Stark leaves his ego at the door, and asks probing and clarifying questions to the subject in a genuine effort to learn as much about the guest as possible, and guests are allowed to present their case. It results in the audience having a more thorough understanding of the interviewee, and at the end of the day everyone can make up their own mind.

Since Robert has interviewed many prominent AltRight figures in a friendly or neutral capacity, many people have mistakenly applied the label to him as well. In fact, it would be an error to attempt to shoehorn Stark's political views into just about any ideological label. This is because ultimately Robert Stark is an artist. As an artist, his politics are aesthetically driven. This is why he's so fascinated with topics like architecture. He ultimately has a mental picture of the type of society he wishes to live in. To the extent specific political policies lend themselves to realizing that vision, he may support them. To the extent they present as obstacles to the transformation of that vision into reality, he may often oppose them. In the cases where he does hold an affinity for certain political convictions, those tend to be secondary and at the margins of his sketchbook of the world and rooted in either his own experential observable reality or a casual ojective analysis after exposure to multiple viewpoints, witnessing failed predictions etc.

I'm thankful for the opportunities Robert has provided me. He has been at the forefront of those taking an interest in helping me promote my work, and through my association with him, I've met an incredible amount of interesting people (as well as a handful of lunatics.) Though it may have began as a simple podcast, The Stark Truth has become the central hub for an eclectic assortment of underground literary figures, politically incorrect weirdos and depraved human oddities that may never have found each other otherwise.

As I mentioned at the beginning, our trip to Las Vegas took place during the summer of 2016. It was a high point for alternative political movements and the salad days of the AltRight as an emerging, little known force in the political landscape. It was a time when these movements and factions were steadily gaining influence but were still unknown enough among the mainstream establishment to be largely left alone. It almost seems like another lifetime compared to now (only two years later at the time of this writing.) The Trump presidential campaign was in full swing, and Robert and I made a point to stop by the Trump International Hotel for our own little photo op. Yes, these were both innocent and promising times. I had just recently quit my soul crushing corporate social media job and decided I was never going back to work at any real job ever again. In a fevered frenzy, I'd also managed to finish writing "Beatnik Fascism" and was eager to set copies of it loose upon unsuspecting masses. For his part, Robert was toying with the idea of running for office in California. I still hope that someday he will, and that once elected, he successfully implements a plan to convert Catalina Island into Vapor Island. Don't underestimate him.

## About The Authors

**R**obert **Stark** is an American journalist and political commentator. You can visit his podcast at www.starktruthradio.com.

**F**rancis **Nally** is a blogger, Youtuber, musician, and avant-garde artist. He is known by his internet name, "pilleater."

**B**randon **Adamson** is a writer and artist, who currently resides in Phoenix Arizona. He has been writing since 1995, and his works has appeared in many magazines, blogs, and literary journals over the years.

www.ingramcontent.com/pod-product-compliance
Lightning Source LLC
LaVergne TN
LVHW011349080426
835511LV00005B/215